earth's echo

earth's echo
Sacred Encounters With Nature

Robert M. Hamma

A sacred and awe-inspiring book.
Annie Dillard, author of *Pilgrim at Tinker Creek*

 SORIN BOOKS   Notre Dame, IN

To my family

who have been so supportive of me,

especially Nancy, Jerry, and Sue Hamma,

and Chris Tessarowicz.

© 2002 by Robert M. Hamma

www.sorinbooks.com

International Standard Book Number: 1-893732-46-0

Cover photo by Imagebank

Cover and text design by Katherine Robinson Coleman

Text photos by www.comstock.com

Printed and bound in the United States of America.

Library of Congress Cataloging-in-Publication Data

Hamma, Robert M.
Earth's echo : sacred encounters with nature / Robert M. Hamma.
        p. cm.
Includes bibliographical references.
ISBN 1-893732-46-0 (pbk.)
1. Nature--Religious aspects--Christianity. I. Title.
BT695.5 .H35 2002
231.7--dc21

                                              2001004616
                                                   CIP

Those who dwell

among the beauties and mysteries of the earth

are never alone or weary of life. . . .

Those who contemplate the beauty of the earth

find reserves of strength

that will endure as long as life lasts.

Rachel Carson
The Sense of Wonder

contents

This book would not have been possible without the support and guidance of many family members, friends, and colleagues. Among those who read the book in early drafts and offered suggestions and creative ideas were: Belden Lane of the University of St. Louis, Judith Anne Beattie, C.S.C., Chris Tessarowicz, and Sharon Schneider.

I am especially grateful for the support of those at Sorin Books: thanks to Publisher Frank Cunningham and John Kirvan for their helpful suggestions, to Dan Driscoll for his careful, sensitive editing, to Pat McGeary, Mary Andrews, and all those in the marketing department who work so hard to get the word out.

To my wife, Kathy Schneider, who always encourages, supports, and enriches my writing with her perspectives, and to my children, Peter, Christine, and Sarah, whose love of nature teaches me so much—I am grateful for your love and your presence in my life.

ONE

reading the book of nature

In the summer nights of my boyhood, when my dad and I would spread a blanket out on the lawn and lie down on our backs, the sky was darker and the stars brighter. I recognized all the summer constellations easily then. I loved watching the long elliptical shape of Scorpio rise, followed by the teapot of Sagittarius. Somehow, I don't remember mosquitoes back then, just the chirping of the katydids and the endless flow of the Milky Way.

Now that I am a man—or as my kids would say, "old"—I treasure those moments. Not only because they recall memories of time together with my dad and the beginning of a lifelong love of stargazing, but also because they gave me a spiritual foundation. Naturally, I didn't think of it that way then, nor would I have cited it when I studied theology. But today I find that one of the richest and most enduring sources of spirituality in my life is nature in all its forms—from stars to starfish.

While a love for nature has always been a part of my life, today I am discovering that the experiences of awe, beauty, and harmony that are so much a part of my appreciation of nature are spiritual in their own right. I'm learning to appreciate that nature is not simply the setting in which the presence of God is encountered, it is, in itself, a form of divine presence. I am only now beginning to try to express in language the mystery that has always been there, but remained unnamed. Perhaps something is indeed lost when we attempt to capture such mystery in words. But for me, the verbal expression of the mystery has led me to a new appreciation of what was inchoately present in my childhood.

Chet Raymo, a science and nature writer for *The Boston Globe,* writes about his rediscovery of the divine in nature in his book *Natural Prayers:*

> All of my life has been a relearning to pray—a letting go of incantational magic, petition, and vain repetition "Me Lord, me," instead of watching attentively for the light that burns at the center of every star, every cell, every living creature, every human heart.

For many of us, this appreciation of the sacred dimension of nature requires a change of perspective. Although we may have an appreciation for the role of nature in our spirituality, it is often limited. Nature may serve as a refuge for us, a place to go to get away from the pressures and distractions of our ordinary lives. We may find that nature's beauty or grandeur inspires us, that the beauty of creation reminds us of the Creator. But is there more to it than that?

participating in the divine

Many of the world's great religious traditions would agree that there is more. The religions of both East and West would concur that nature can be seen as a metaphor of the spiritual life. In this first level of recognition, the ordinary processes of nature illustrate for us the presence or the action of God. God is like a rock, or like the sea, or like the rain in the desert, the psalms say. Jesus compares the coming of God's reign to the sprouting of a seed. And Lao Tzu, the Taoist philosopher, compares the flow of the river to the soul's progress.

A second level of appreciation for the sacred dimension of nature begins with a sense of participation in nature. It is the recognition that nature involves us, that we are part of it. There is a deep divide in contemporary consciousness between the human and the natural. We speak of "getting back to nature," or worse, "man against nature," as if we were not a part of it, as if it were something for us to conquer. This patriarchal attitude toward nature has indeed led to the destruction of countless forms of life and robbed so many of the sense of belonging in the world. Like the birds, like the clouds, like the breeze, we are a part of nature. Indeed, we are made of the same stuff as the animals and the trees. The same energy that is alive in them is alive in us.

When we recognize this we realize that our hierarchies and distinctions among different forms of life have their limits. In focusing on the differences between forms of life, we have often forgotten that life is one, that there is a community of life. Thus when we harm various ecosystems, we harm the humanity that is a part of the web of life. The essayist Scott Russell Sanders has observed,

All life rises from the same source, and so does all fellow feeling, whether the fellows move on two legs or four, on scaly bellies or feathered wings. If we care for only human needs, we betray the land; if we care only for the earth and its wild offspring, we betray our own kind.

This recognition of our participation in the natural world awakens in us a new sense of community and a broader sense of compassion.

Just as the most fragile species are hurt most by the loss of habitat, and the poisoning of the waters, so in our human community the poor, those already on the margins, are most affected by the wanton destruction of the natural world. This awareness of our participation in nature can, if we are willing, break down the hubris that has allowed us to think of ourselves as superior to other forms of life, of having the inherent right to do what we please with them.

If we are a part of nature, then the mystery at work in the depths of our souls and the mystery at work in the natural world are parts of the same reality. Just as the experience of communion that is integral to love reveals to us the presence of the divine in what is most deeply human, so too the experience of communion with nature reveals to us the divine presence at the heart of nature.

This recognition of our participation in nature and our essential unity with nature leads to the next level of awareness: that nature reveals God and is a sacred presence in itself. It is not new to say that nature reveals the divine. In my childhood stargazing I experienced a sense of wonder, awe, beauty, and wholeness. The universe revealed God to me, though at the time I may not have named it as such. Such numinous experiences are the foundation of all religions, and the experience is sometimes described as cosmic revelation—the recognition that all of creation points to a Creator.

So while the assertion that nature reveals God is not surprising, the claim that nature is a sacred presence in itself may be. To say this is to say that nature does not merely point to God or reveal God the way a painting reveals the artist; it is to claim even more. Mystics in the great religious traditions, from Christianity to Buddhism, have often made the assertion that we in our humanity participate in a real way in the life of God. If we may dare to claim some participation in the life of God, some presence of divinity within us, can we not also say that nature too participates in divinity and that God is present in it? "If you wish to know the divine," the Buddha said, "feel the wind on your face and the warm sun on your hand."

I know that these experiences are true: The song of the cardinal at dawn is a word of God spoken to me, and God is in that word. A plunge into the ocean is an exhilarating immersion into life, and God is in the sea. A hug from my daughter Sarah as she throws herself at me with abandon fills me with joy, and God is in her embrace. If we can say these things, can we not also say that God is in the mountain, in the forest, and in the desert?

I have arrived at these convictions in a simple way: by spending time in the natural world and by paying attention. As the poet Mary Oliver says, "To pay attention is our endless and proper work." The natural world in which I try to pay attention is simply the world around me. I don't live in the mountains or on the shore. I live at the edge of a small city. While I love the mountains and the shore and go there whenever I can, there is plenty to see right here. If we think only of nature as some wild or idyllic place, we'll spend most of our lives waiting to get there. But the natural world is right here, and as Henry David Thoreau said, "My profession is always to be alert, to find God in nature."

Paying attention to nature involves first noticing what we see. When looking at a great work of art, teachers sometimes advise their students to write down everything they see. This practice has a way of slowing down the eye and helping it to see more. This can be a helpful way of heightening our attentiveness to nature as well. Sometimes what we see can be too much for us to absorb. On those occasions it can be helpful to frame the scene and focus on just a part of it. One just sits and observes what can be seen through a window, or one focuses on a particular tree or a certain squirrel and follows it.

Some people have a naturalist's inclination, wanting to know the name of each thing and to be able to classify it. Others may have the artist's eye with its awareness of light, form, and texture. These can be helpful, and for some they are the way for them to discover the divine presence in the world. But there is another way of paying attention, a way in which we are content to simply be there, without a desire to learn or to know, without a desire to capture the essence of the moment and give it artistic expression. We are there simply to be there, and to be aware of the divinity of that place in that moment.

The ways of the artist and the naturalist are only two examples of different ways of paying attention that can all lead to a contemplative awareness of nature. In this contemplative awareness, the particularity of nature, of all that we see, gives rise to the perception of the universal. In *The Contemplative Heart,* James Finley writes, "As we give ourselves over to this gazing there rises up in the . . . concreteness of all that is seen, an intimate vision of the all-in-one, one-in-all nature of reality." Whether by astute observation or by simply being there, our attention opens us to the realization that all things are interconnected and that the divine presence is found in each one.

a path toward awareness

Paying attention is hard work; contemplative insight is not like an apple we can pluck from a tree. Adopting the right attitude is a necessary first step. That attitude is not one of goal setting but of patience. It is an attitude that simply being there is enough. Setting goals for maintaining heightened awareness or expecting insights to come can lead to disappointment when the inevitable distractions take over, or when we "get nothing out of it." It helps to know that we are not the first people to ever attempt this, and that there are paths that others have trod before us.

This book employs one such well-worn path. It is an ancient method of reflection called *lectio divina,* or sacred reading. Rooted in Judaism, it evolved into its classic Christian form in monasticism. Today it is practiced not only by monks and nuns, but also by people everywhere of Christian, Muslim, Buddhist, and secular background. Indeed anyone interested in discovering the presence of the divine in their lives can profit from this simple four-step process.

As the phrase "sacred reading" indicates, the most common understanding of this practice is as a method of prayer based on the reading of scripture.

But we should be careful not to interpret "reading" too narrowly. For books, in fact, were something of a rarity for those who developed this process. Even in monasteries, books were scarce. As the Trappist monk M. Basil Pennington has pointed out, "For centuries *lectio* was much more a matter of hearing [rather than reading] the Word of God." The word that was the basis of reflection was proclaimed in worship, chanted in choir, or read aloud during the silent meals. While the word was most often scriptural, other sacred texts were read as well—commentaries on the scripture, treatises of revered writers, the sayings of the founders. The spoken word was heard, remembered, and carried forward for reflection later.

The word was not only heard, but could be seen as well. Medieval cathedrals surrounded worshipers with a host of visual images designed to lead to meditation. Stained-glass windows depicted scenes from the Bible, magnificent rose windows captured the light and drew viewers into their mandala-like patterns, the sweeping lines of the architecture drew all eyes heavenward, and the statues reminded worshipers of the exemplary lives of the saints. Thus it is certainly in keeping with the Christian tradition to recognize nature—or as the monastics would say, creation—as a subject for sacred reading. As Pennington says:

> The whole of creation bespeaks its Maker. As the Greeks would say, the whole of

creation is full of *logoi,* "little words," that give expression to *Logos*, the Word. I can stand on my bluff overlooking the Pearl River Delta and wonder at it all: the creation of God and humans, the beauty of the sky, the sea, the islands, the exuberant energy of metropolis Hong Kong—it all speaks of God, gives expression to the Word.

There is a story about the hermit Antony who lived in the Egyptian desert during the third century. One day a philosopher approached him and asked what he would do if he could no longer read the scripture. To this Antony replied: "My book, sir philosopher, is the nature of created things, and it is always on hand when I wish to read it." The early twentieth century Sufi teacher Hazrat Inayat Khan expressed the same insight this way: "There is only one sacred manuscript, the sacred manuscript of nature, which alone can enlighten any reader."

The practice of sacred reading consists of four movements or steps: reading, meditation, prayer, and contemplation. This book employs the four traditional movements in a new way, though one that is in keeping with its ancient formulation. The "text" that we will read is the "book of nature," the words are those of nature writers. Naturalists, scientists, adventurers, novelists, poets—all have written about nature, recording their observations, capturing the magnificence of a moment, offering insights gained from their encounters with the natural world. We will read passages from diverse writers like the poet Walt Whitman, the oceanographer Robert Kunzig, the pioneer of the ecological movement Rachel Carson, and the novelist Ursula Hegi. Their writings are sacred because their subject, the earth, is sacred. Their words are inspired not only because of their scientific or literary gifts, but also because of the rich spirituality they exhibit in their experience of nature. And most important, it is a sacred process because of what happens in us.

a sacred reading of nature

This book calls the first step of the process **Paying Attention**. In reading the words of these writers as a sacred text, we raise our attention to another level. We see nature through their eyes, but hopefully with new freshness in our own. Why not simply go outside and observe nature for ourselves? Why not indeed! Their words do not replace our own need to pay attention to nature, but may enable us to see more, to see differently, or to see anew.

Our second step in the process of sacred reading is **Pondering**. As we join these writers in the process of paying attention, their considerations give rise to thoughts of our own. Pondering nature opens many paths of reflection to us. Our memory may be stirred. When we read, for example, a description of the tide coming in, we may remember a time when we stood on the shore and observed the rising of the tide. Through memory we return to that moment and allow ourselves to discover what it may say to us now.

Or perhaps our imagination is awakened. In our mind's eye we place ourselves on the shore and create the scene evoked by the passage. We picture the waves rolling in, we hear them, we may even smell or taste their brine. We place ourselves there and discover what the voice of nature has to say to us.

Sometimes our pondering of nature may lead us to realize that what is going on in nature is like something that is going on within us. The rising of the tide speaks to us of something rising up within. This comparison can offer insights about our lives and lead us to take certain steps for change or growth.

At other times our reflection on nature may stir a moral response within us. Certain attitudes or dispositions within us may be exposed as inadequate. We may find ourselves indignant or even outraged at an evil we suddenly see. Or, we may be urged to take some action to work for change, to deepen our sense of compassion.

Finally, we may have no apparent response on any of these levels. We may simply just want to be in that place at that moment without any active use of our mind or stirring of emotion. One ancient monastic writer called meditation the "rocking of the heart." Like a boat swaying gently on the swells, we simply allow the presence of nature to carry us. Another monk compared this process of meditation to a cow chewing her cud. The cow is not looking for any insights, not feeling great consolation, not making any plans; she's just chewing. We may just want to ponder the tide rising—nothing more, nothing less.

No one of these ways of pondering nature is better than another. All we need do is simply to follow the impulses we sense within us and stay with the process as faithfully as we can. Let the ponderings in this book encourage your own efforts at reflection. Allow these passages to speak to you on various levels. They may conjure up memories, hopes, joys, and fears. They may spur your imagination, produce insights, or call you to change. Sometimes you may just want to carry them around with you for stretches at a time without any specific response, simply because you enjoyed their company. Perhaps my meditations will speak to you, but more important, I hope they will encourage you in your own.

In the third step of this process, we offer a **Response** to the One whose voice we have heard. Our response comes spontaneously and it will depend on what we have heard. We may be joyful or sad, angry or enthused. Our aim in this movement is not a particular type of response, it is to recognize our heart's desire in response to the "word" and to express it in a personal way.

In the traditional method of sacred reading, this step was called prayer, expressing perhaps praise or gratitude, seeking help, or asking forgiveness. If we encounter the divine presence in ourselves or in nature, we may wish to respond to that presence in our own words. The responses in this section express my way of responding to the voice of God as I have heard it through this process. Sometimes they are reflective of a sense of incompleteness, of questioning. Sometimes they address a presence in nature that has touched me. Sometimes they address the Holy One who is greater than our hearts, who cannot be contained in any thing, who is All in All. Perhaps they will capture some of your spirit's yearning; perhaps they will lead you to pray.

You may find that the best way for you to respond is not verbally, as suggested here, but physically—in art or dance, by playing music or going for a run. Whatever form your response takes, let it gather the pieces together, not necessarily seeking a final resolution, but as a way of summing up the inner movement of your spirit and carrying it forward.

The traditional name for the fourth step of the process is contemplation. Contemplation begins where all our efforts at meditation and prayer end and we find ourselves caught up in the movement and presence of God. Such an experience is a gift, not something we can cause or accomplish. We can engage in spiritual practices that open us to such experiences, but we cannot create them. All we can do, as the mystics say, is dry the wood and stack it carefully so that when the match is laid, it catches fire.

Here this step is called **Surrendering**. A brief aphorism has been selected that speaks to each passage and provides a thought to carry us through the day. The words may serve as a type of mantra, or may inspire you to create a mantra of your own. Recollection of the phrase or repetition of the mantra may serve as a way to cultivate a contemplative awareness within us. Doing so is a process of surrendering our hearts to the One who has called us.

finding patterns

Each part of this book covers a certain natural region: the shore, the forest, the desert, the river, and the mountain. I chose these biomes because they are what I know best, they are places that, to varying degrees, I have experienced and appreciated. You may want to focus on other regions as well.

As I engaged in this process of reflection, I was struck by the endless variety of nature. When I looked, for example, at rivers I saw that no two rivers were alike. They varied from their origin to their end, and the same place in the river was different from one day to the next. My aim was not to reflect on the various ways a river might manifest itself along its journey to the sea, but rather to reflect on the different ways that a river engaged me. In doing so, I found certain types of responses emerging within me, not only to the river, but to all the different environments that I experienced.

Each of the chapters of this book will lead you on an exploration of eight kinds of experiences of nature. We begin by simply **encountering** this aspect of nature. Do you remember the first time you experienced an ocean, or a snow-capped mountain, or a desert? In our first step we simply immerse ourselves into a part of nature, seeking to see it as if for the first time. A **sense of nature's beauty** and a **feeling of comfort** are among the first responses we have when we immerse ourselves in nature. These are the second and third steps we take.

But there are dimensions of nature that are not consoling. They may be overwhelming or frightening. When we reflect on the majesty of Mt. Rainier or the raw power of Niagara Falls, we are humbled. When this sobering sense of our smallness expresses itself in wonder or praise, we call it awe. When it produces fear or dread within us, we dwell on our sense of powerlessness. These are our fourth and fifth steps: **standing in awe** and **recognizing our powerlessness**.

In our experience of nature, we sometimes sense an invitation. It is not enough simply to admire it, receive its comfort, or be reminded of our place in the world. Nature is not simply an object for us to reflect on. It is a presence, a subject with whom we interact. If we are attentive to nature, we discover that it asks something of us. In our sixth step we **listen to the call** of the river or the desert and seek to discern what is being said. In our seventh step, we seek to respond to that call by **moving in rhythm** with nature and allowing that pattern to permeate our lives.

With our eighth and final step, we come full circle. We leave our exploration of some part of nature aware of the ways that we have been touched by both the light and the darkness. We seek to keep its call alive and to move in its rhythm by **carrying nature within us**.

What is the ultimate purpose of this practice of sacred reading of nature? What will happen to us if we engage in it regularly? In traditional religious language, the aim of sacred reading is a purification of the heart, a conversion. Immersed in the word, it gradually shapes one's life and permeates one's consciousness.

A sacred reading of nature can have a similar affect on us. The word we might choose today to describe it is transformation. It is a process of change that occurs in us at many levels: intellectually, psychologically, spiritually. As we begin to think about nature differently, our experience of it changes, and our appreciation of its deepest dimensions is enlivened. This internal process leads to a new consciousness. Out of that consciousness emerge new values, new activities, new commitments. Transformation is an ongoing process. We are always discovering new things about ourselves, trying to discern what is the right way to live in our world, how to use our gifts and our resources.

We live in a time when human activity has placed nature under unprecedented assault. Even as we come to see the presence of the divine in the natural world, we cannot help seeing the destructive force of our human hands. Global warming, climate change, pollution—indeed every environmental problem we may name springs in part from the demystification of nature, from the loss of its sacred dimension in our consciousness. This book has emerged out of my conviction that the environmental crisis before us has spiritual roots. But if this is so, then there is also reason for hope, since the solution will begin on a spiritual level as well. Effecting real change begins with the transformation of the human heart. Only then can we hope for some lasting achievement.

When we begin to recognize that this world we inhabit, this universe through which we journey, is indeed a sacred reality, a divine presence, we will have found a lasting source of vision and strength for both our personal and social lives.

the shore

1. Encountering the Shore

paying attention

Like the sea itself, the shore fascinates us who return to it, the place of our dim ancestral beginnings. In the recurrent rhythms of tides and surf and in the varied life of the tidelines there is the obvious attraction of movement and change and beauty. There is also, I am convinced, a deeper fascination born of inner meaning and significance.

When we go down to the low-tide line we enter a world that is as old as the earth itself—the primeval meeting place of the elements of earth and water, a place of compromise and conflict and eternal change. For us as living creatures it has special meaning as a place in or near which some entity that could be distinguished as Life first drifted in shallow waters—reproducing, evolving, yielding that endlessly varied stream of living things that has surged through time and space to occupy the earth.

Rachel Carson

The sea has attracted me for as long as I can remember. Born and raised on Long Island, I have returned again and again to its Atlantic shore—to Long Beach and Point Lookout, to the west end of Jones Beach and Fire Island, to Sagaponack and to Montauk. Throughout my life the sounds, the smells, the tastes, and of course the beauty of the shore have exerted a tidal pull on me. Despite the ever changing visage of the sea, I find a constancy there. In that endless change there is permanence. Each time I return I realize that I am the one who has changed. And each time I find a never failing source of strength and hope in "the recurrent rhythms of tide and surf."

The movement, the change, and the beauty of the sea offers us an "obvious attraction." But there is also, as Carson says, "a deeper fascination." The obvious attraction of movement, change, and beauty leads me to examine the dynamics of "compromise, conflict, and eternal change," not only at this elemental meeting place of earth and ocean, but in my heart and soul. In the give and take of sand and sea I recognize the giving and taking of love and friendship, the reconciling compromise that unites what was broken. In the conflictual crashing of the waves upon the shore I hear the pain-filled cries and the unfulfilled longings—my own, my loved ones', and those of the poor and the oppressed. In the eternally changing face of the beach, I touch the ever changing lines of my dreams, my hopes. Ever changing, yet still the same.

As life once emerged in these frothing, swirling waters, new dreams, new hopes, and new possibilities continue to emerge within me.

responding

At this elemental meeting place of earth and
    sea and sky,
I sense your call to look inward
even as I gaze outward at the horizon.

The waves wash over my feet
and I sink gradually into the sand,
rooting me in the earth and the sea.

Simply by being here
I know I am part
of the rhythm of the tide and the energy of the
    surf.

I am a unique expression
of the endless and varied stream of living
    things
whose life is your life.

With each wave I sense
the giving and the taking, the tears and the
     laughter,
the longing and the fulfillment of all living
     things.

With each wave I am touched
by the constancy of your presence.
And I dare to believe that all shall be well.

surrendering

For the mighty wind arises roaring seaward, and
I go.

Alfred, Lord Tennyson

paying attention

When I think back to my first days here, I realize how greedily I collected. My pockets bulged with wet shells. The beach was covered with beautiful shells. I could not let one go by unnoticed. I could not even walk head up, looking out to sea, for fear of missing something precious at my feet. . . . But after all the pockets were stretched and damp and the bookcase shelves filled and the window ledges covered, I began to drop my acquisitiveness. I began to discard from my possessions, to select.

One cannot collect all the beautiful shells on the beach. One can collect only a few, and they are more beautiful if they are few. One moon shell is more impressive than three. There is only one moon in the sky. One double sunrise is an event, six are a succession, like a week of school days. Gradually one discards and keeps just the perfect specimen; not necessarily a rare shell, but a perfect one of its kind. One sets it apart by itself, ringed around by space—like the island.

For it is only framed in space that beauty blooms. Only in space are events and objects and people unique and significant—and therefore beautiful.

Anne Morrow Lindbergh

Outside the back door of my house is a plastic bag filled with shells that my daughter and I collected months ago at the beach. They'll stay there till I persuade her to take care of them or do something with them myself. They are all beautiful, big clamshells that we gathered on a walk one afternoon. I don't think she knows what to do with them now, and neither do I.

As we walked along the beach that day we were like Anne Morrow Lindbergh—unable to look up at the sea for fear of missing something precious. But unlike her, we haven't made the move yet from acquisitiveness to selectivity. What we need to do is find one that we like the best and put it someplace special. Perhaps its beauty will be in its perfect form, or maybe it will be because we remember something funny or unique about finding that shell. Once we select our shell and put it in its own place, we'll remember that day—the warmth of the sun on our backs, the way the water glistened in the late afternoon, the sound of the gulls above us— whenever we look at it.

The beauty of the shore can be overwhelming. We want to absorb it all, to take it all in, to hold on to it like that bag of shells. But beauty cannot be possessed like that. We can't hold on to all the beautiful moments, the beautiful people, or the beautiful things in our lives. Only by contemplating what is beautiful can it become a part of us.

Contemplation is sometimes called a "long loving look." When we absorb something that way, then it is always there.

"In framed space . . . beauty blooms," Lindbergh says. Only by creating space in our lives can we recognize the beauty that is there. In contemplating the one shell rather than the many, we discover the beauty of them all. Once we have experienced that, we have only to look upon that shell reverently to see all the beauty of the shore before us.

responding

Mostly I walk with my head down,
gathering shells,
looking for the best ones,
staying focused on the task.

I have the collector's penchant
for keeping things organized,
knowing my priorities,
expanding my holdings.

Even when surrounded by beauty
I have a goal:
take it all in,
don't miss a part.

Help me to stop
and take a long, loving look
at just one shell,
at just one smile.

Teach me how
to put a frame around a moment,
to pause reverently,
to see simply.

surrendering

The earth shall be complete to the one who shall
be complete.

Walt Whitman

3. The Comfort of the Shore

paying attention

Skirting the point lies a confused mass of granite boulders, many man-sized and larger. Crevasses, depressions and cavities hold hundreds of tide pools—each a different world, each worth exploring. Without realizing it I began to fall into a mood of well-being—my family around me, a time of rest, reading, writing, photography, conversation. I found this contentment reflected in the tide pools as I scrambled over the rocks each day, trying to see into them all.

I jumped from rock to rock, looking deep inside the pools they held, lying on my belly on dry rocks, squatting on algae slick platforms by the lower pools. Each pool—some washed more, some less, by waves—held a different community. The sea left some alone for varying lengths of time, some not at all; habitats differed in turbulence, salinity variation, amounts and kinds of food. I looked down and in, occasionally surprising my own face in reflection, looking into my eyes. Sky and clouds below me and above, I dove and climbed at the same time. A gull's reflection filled a mussel pool high above the low tide mark—black and blue mussels; delicate, pink corallina; green cladopora bright in sunlight then in sudden shadow. The gull landed beside me and joined others feeding in small pools under ledges and in shallow crevasses. Unafraid, a dozen herring gulls surrounded me, picking food from the pools.

Douglas Carlson

pondering

There is great comfort in knowing that I am not alone. Because I have the great gift in my life of being known and loved by my wife, it is comforting simply to be together. We need not talk about anything significant, sometimes we don't talk at all. We're simply together.

Douglas Carlson describes a similar comfort in this passage. On vacation with his family on the Maine coast, a sense of well-being comes over him. It springs from the sense of belonging to an intimate community, with time for renewal and introspection. But it also comes from discovering himself to be a part of other communities as well. While other vacationers were busy looking at lighthouses and breakers, he was slithering around on the rocks. In each of the pools he examines, he finds "a different community." He examines each of the endless variety of habitats containing different life forms.

As he gazes into a pool he surprises himself with his own reflection. He sees himself there amidst the mussels and the corallina. As he looks at these creatures, he looks into his own eyes and discovers he belongs to this community too. Companioned by a gull, he soon finds himself a part of the flock as he squats on the rocks sharing their participation in that community of life.

The comfort of the shore is in knowing that we are not alone, that we are part of a multifaceted communion of life. In us the rocks and the sea, the mussels and the gulls—all of creation—has come to consciousness. In our knowing and being known, in our loving and being loved, we are one not only with each other, but with all creatures, all things.

responding

Praise to you
for my brother the gull,
my sister the tide,
my father the boulder,
my mother the sea.

Glory to the maker
of the black and blue mussels,
the delicate pink corallina,
the bright green cladopora,
they are my brothers and sisters too.

Thanks for the people who share my life,
knowing and being known,
loving and being loved,
one with creation, one with each other,
one with you.

⌒surrendering

I am that living and fiery essence of the divine substance. . . . I shine in the water, I burn in the sun and the moon and the stars.

Hildegard of Bingen

4. Standing in Awe

paying attention

As the structure of the atom has been unraveled in the twentieth century, so has the structure of the water molecule. It accounts for water's remarkable properties, which is to say that it accounts—in the sense of being a necessary condition—for the most distinctive properties of our planet, including the fact that it is inhabited.

Water exists because it solves a problem oxygen has. An oxygen atom has six negatively charged electrons in its outer shell, orbiting the positively charged nucleus, but it has room for and longs to be filled by two more. Two hydrogen atoms donate the missing electrons and are thereby bound tightly to the oxygen. The eight electrons form four pairs . . . that separate as far as they can. . . . The result is a four cornered molecule, a tetrahedron. Projecting from two corners are hydrogen nuclei, that is individual protons. The other two corners are naked electron pairs. The protons give one side of the water molecule a positive electric charge, while the electrons make the other side negative.

This electric polarization has profound consequences. The naked electron pairs attract their opposite numbers, hydrogen nuclei in other water molecules. . . . Each molecule can join hands with a neighbor at the four corners of the pyramid, grabbing a hydrogen at two corners and a pair of oxygen electrons at the other two. The liaison is fleeting though; it is like the passing touch exchanged by dancers in a quadrille . . . as they constantly change partners.

Robert Kunzig

$\smile$ pondering

A s we stand on the shore we often associate the awesome majesty and power of the sea with its vastness or its destructive power. But perhaps we should turn our attention to the water itself. The most awesome thing about the sea is the very existence of water itself. For without water there can be no life.

"Water exists because it solves a problem oxygen has," Robert Kunzig says. Out of this incompleteness life emerges. Hydrogen, the simplest of atoms, fuses with oxygen and forms the basis of all of the complex life structures. This fusion does not create a simple and harmonious entity. Rather it forms a highly polarized molecule that is always in flux, always engaged in the dance of creation. Water molecules change partners "billions of times a second," Kunzig adds.

Billions of times a second.

This fusion, called the hydrogen bond, is what accounts for the many states of H_2O—as liquid, solid, and gas. It is why a wave can crash on the shore casting droplets high in the air, spraying mist on my face and salt on my lips, while bathing my feet in foam and bubbles.

I stand in awe before the immensity and power of the vast ocean . . . I stand in awe before the genius and perfection of each water molecule.

responding

You are the immensity and power of
    the vast ocean.
You are the genius and perfection of
    each of its molecules.

You are permanence.
You are change.

You are the music.
You are the dance.

You hold all things together
by the power of your love.

surrendering

You are a droplet of water from an infinite ocean of consciousness.

Haji Bahaudin

5. Powerless Before It

paying attention

Sound of surf in these autumnal dunes—the continuousness of it, sound of endless charging, endless fulfillment and dissolution, endless fecundity, and endless death. I have been trying to study out the mechanics of that endless resonance. The dominant note is the great spilling crash made by each arriving wave. It may be hollow and booming, it may be heavy and churning, it may be a tumbling roar. The second fundamental sound is the wild seething cataract roar of the wave's dissolution and the rush of the foaming waters up the beach—the second sound *diminuendo*. The third fundamental sound is the endless dissolving hiss of the inmost slides of foam. The first two sounds reach the ear as a unisonance—the booming impact of the tons of water and the wild roar of the up-rushing blending—and this mingled sound dissolves into the foaming bubble hissing of the third. Above the tumult, like birds, fly wisps of watery noise, splashes and counter splashes, whispers, seethings, slaps, and chucklings. An overtone sound of the other breakers, mingled with a general rumbling, fells earth and sea and air.

Henry Beston

As a boy I loved to body surf. The experience of catching a wave and being thrust forward by it, of free falling as it broke, of bouncing through its tumult and roar, was for me the ultimate experience of unity with nature and the transcendent power at work in it. I lived for the days when a stiff offshore breeze would peak the crests of the waves, sending their spray seaward upon me as I stood waiting for just the right one to ride.

At about the age of twelve I remember arriving at the beach well before noon with my family on just such a perfect day. As I hurried through my chores of planting the umbrella and spreading the blanket, I was eager for the adventures of these waves. Then I looked up to see my much younger brother struggling to stay afloat well beyond the breakers.

My father and I dashed into the surf and quickly retrieved him. He was completely calm, unfazed and unaware of the real danger he had been exposed to. But for the first time I became aware of the dark potency of the sea. The risk of entering it was suddenly more than the skinned knees that I proudly displayed when I caught a wave that was a little too big and wild and was pounded to the bottom. As I entered the sea that day, my joyful abandon was just a bit tempered.

The power of the sea is the power of life and the power of death. As I stand on the shore and listen to the pattern of each wave's crash and roar and hiss that Henry Beston described so beautifully, I reflect on the pattern of fulfillment and dissolution, of fecundity and death, as they repeat themselves in my life. Each day, indeed each moment, I am one with the force of life . . . and I am passing away. In the sea I see life and death not in battle, but as one.

The endless motion of life, varied and strong, confronts me with my powerlessness. I am but a moment of fulfillment and dissolution, an instant of fecundity and death. But how marvelous, how unrepeatable is my life. Each of us is an absolutely distinct expression of the surging energy of life. Our growing and aging, our giving birth and dying, play a song that has never been heard before.

As we stand powerless before the crash and roar and hiss of the sea, we are carried by its endlessly alluring rhythm.

responding

Crescendo, diminuendo,
the rhythm of my life flows on,
part of the song of the universe.

You who hold life and death together,
giver of this marvelous gift,
singer of this song,

give me the courage to let go
of my need to be always in control,
and give me the trust to accept my ultimate
    powerlessness.

Restore the joy of my youth,
not in naiveté, but with the awareness that
I am one with the force of life . . . and I am
    passing away.

Give me ears to hear your voice,
grant me courage to live freely,
and eyes to see you in all things.

surrendering

All your waves and your billows have gone over
me.

Psalm 42:7

6. The Call of the Shore

For ten years I have migrated from beach shack to cabin, moving along the shore like the native tribes that once encircled all of Puget Sound. But unlike the first people who loved this wild serpentine body of cold water, my encampments have changed with the whim of my landlords rather than with the seasons. Somehow, mixed up in my blood of Seminole, Swede, and French Canadian Indian is my belief that I may never own land even if one day I might be able to afford it. Ownership implies possession; as much as I revere this inland sea, she will never belong to me. Why not, then, belong to her?

Belong. As a child, the word mesmerized me. Because my father's forestry work moved us every other year—from southern piney woods to soaring Montana spruce to High Sierra fir—the landscape seemed in motion. To *be long* in one place was to take deep root like other settled folk, or like the trees themselves, the Standing People, as my father called them. There was also the elegant and open-hearted *longing* in belonging that even today, after a decade settling on the shores of Puget Sound, hasn't been sated in me. After I have lived a long life on this beach, I hope that someone might someday say,

"She belonged here," as much as the purple starfish that cling to the rock crevices covered in algae fur.

Brenda Peterson

pondering

I must admit that I often dream of owning some land by the shore. Living less than an hour from Lake Michigan, I think it would be wonderful to have a place to go to throughout the year, to let the ever changing patterns of the lake and dunes become a part of me. Brenda Peterson's words, "I may never own land even if one day I might afford it," challenge me.

What do I really want? Is it a cottage with a view? A private beach? No, what I long for is not ownership, but the opportunity to let the call of the shore sink into my heart more deeply. And what do I need to do that? I need simply to be there. I don't need to win the lottery or write a bestseller to simply put some time aside and go. But I struggle to hear the call of the shore and to respond to it. Would owning a piece of land on the beach change that?

Indeed, the issue is not whether the shore belongs to me, but whether I belong to it. To truly belong there, I must listen to its call, I must make space for an "elegant open-hearted longing" to grow within me. In order to belong to the shore, I must *be long* there.

To what does it call me? Why do I want to be there? What happens to me when I do respond? In one sense the call of the shore for me is a call to take some time away from my life and gain a new perspective. But the shore is not just a place of retreat. It is a place where life's incredible complexity, its constant struggle, its subtle rhythms are ever present for one who looks. The call of the sea is an invitation to live in the present, to see life each day in its richness and diversity. Sometimes it seems easier to live that way around the sea, but I suspect that it would not be so simple once I settled in and the distractions of everyday life took hold.

I can't promise that I'll never own a piece of the shore, but for now, I'll try to practice the kind of attentiveness to life that it calls me to. This way, when I do win the lottery, I'll be ready.

responding

I hear your voice
in the gentle lapping of the waves,
in the breeze as it bends the dune grass,
in the squawking of the gulls.

It stirs in me
an elegant open-hearted longing,
a desire to remain here,
to be entranced by the shore's magic.

It beckons me to stay,
but my life is not here, at the sea's edge
where simplicity seems so easy to find.
Where I belong, it's harder to keep my
    bearings.

Teach me to make a space for longing
in the midst of the noise and clutter.
May the call of the shore
reverberate throughout my life,

inviting me to attentiveness,
teaching me not to grasp,
possessing me with its emptiness,
immersing me in its fullness.

surrendering

Nothing can bring you peace but yourself.

Ralph Waldo Emerson

7. Moving in the Shore's Rhythm

In a pool of sand and silt a starfish had thrust its arms up stiffly and was holding its body away from the stifling mud.

"It's still alive," I ventured.

"Yes," he said, and with a quick yet gentle movement he picked up the star and spun it over my head and far out into the sea. It sank in a burst of spume and the waters roared once more.

"It may live," he said, "if the offshore pull is strong enough."

He spoke gently, and across his bronzed, worn face the light still came and went in subtly altering colors.

"There are not many come this far," I said, groping in a sudden embarrassment for words. "Do you collect?"

"Only like this," he said softly, gesturing amidst the wreckage of the shore. "And only for the living." He stopped again, oblivious of my curiosity and skipped another star neatly across the water.

"The stars," he said, "throw well. One can help them."

He looked full at me with a faint question kindling in his eyes, which seemed to take on the far depths of the sea.

"I do not collect," I said uncomfortably, the wind beating at my garments. "Neither the living nor the dead. I gave it up a long time ago. Death is the only successful collector."

I nodded and walked away, leaving him there upon the dune with that great rainbow ranging up the sky behind him. . . .

Loren Eiseley

pondering

One of the things I love most about long days at the shore is watching the gradual turning of the tide. The tide comes in and sandcastles are swamped, drowsy sunbathers are suddenly awakened. It goes out and the plovers appear, dashing about and pecking away. The detritus of the waves provides treasures aplenty for collecting. Even these simple signs of the tide's turning hint at the drama beneath the rhythm of the sea.

But one must go a bit beyond a lazy afternoon to appreciate its significance. The two men in the encounter described above have "come far" to play a part, each in their own way, in the drama of the tides. Their awkward conversation nevertheless reveals two distinct ways of participating—one might say dancing—to the rhythm of the sea. Loren Eiseley, who once described himself as a "literary naturalist," is not a collector, nor is he a rescuer. His counterpart, whom he calls "the star thrower," does not collect in the normal sense, but "only like this," by returning the faltering starfish to the sea.

Eiseley's parting words, "Death is the only successful collector," seem cynical. Yet as he walks away he notices a great rainbow rising up above the star thrower. A blessing perhaps? A sign of hope?

Who am I in this parable? I wonder. The rescuer who battles the tidal surge? The wizened observer who defers to the powerful forces of nature? And how far have I come in my appreciation of the rhythms of the sea within me?

responding

In the dance of the shore
that ebbs and flows within me
there is a time to hold on,
and a time to let go,
a time to come far,
and a time to hold back
a rising of hope,
and a falling into acceptance.

There is the struggle to preserve life,
and the willingness to hold it in memory,
the effort to resist,
and the inclination to defer
to the pull of the tide,
and the rising of the rainbow.
If only I could learn to dance
and move more smoothly with your rhythm.

surrendering

We are an abyss that only God can fill.

Augustine of Hippo

8. Carrying the Shore Within You

paying attention

Hours, days, in my Long Island youth and early manhood, I haunted the shores of Rockaway or Coney Island, or away east to the Hamptons or Montauk. Once, at the latter place (by the old lighthouse, nothing but sea tossings in sight in every direction as far as the eye could reach), I remember well, I felt that I must one day write a book expressing this liquid, mystic theme. Afterward, I recollect how it came to me that instead of any special lyrical or epical or literary attempt, the seashore should be an invisible *influence*, a pervading gauge and tally for me, in my composition. (Let me give a hint here to young writers. I am not sure but I have unwittingly followed out the same rule with other powers besides sea and shores—avoiding them, in the way of any dead set at poetizing them, as too big for formal handling—quite satisfied if I could indirectly show that we have met and fused, even if only once, but enough—that we have really absorb'd each other and understand each other.)

Walt Whitman

I remember a summer afternoon in late August. The waves rolled gently toward the shore as I swam toward the sun. It hung low in the pale haze of the coming evening. Doing an easy breaststroke, I moved slowly, in no hurry. The light shimmered and danced on the smooth surface of the water. Without the focus of my glasses, it looked to me like a scene from a Monet painting.

Summer was ending, high school would start again soon. But I didn't want to go back to my friends, to the cross country team, to Latin class. I just wanted to stay there, swimming forever into the sun.

Why do I remember that moment now, almost four decades later? Why have I always remembered it and sought to re-create it each time I go for a late afternoon swim? Perhaps it was a moment when, as Whitman says, the ocean and I "really absorb'd each other." I know I sensed myself a part of something bigger, something both gentle and powerful, something that would carry me and draw me always toward the light. It was not a moment of insight or understanding; it was rather a moment filled with longing and peace, strangely coexisting side by side.

It is a moment that is hard to describe, "too big for formal handling." But that sense of being at home in the ocean, and yet being filled with longing for something more is a gift that the sea has blessed me with time and again. I know that in that gracious moment I grasp the truth that I am one with the world, yet always longing for more. It is a truth I carry within me, a "pervading gauge and tally," as Whitman says, by which I measure the degree to which I am in touch with reality.

responding

You are the water that gently holds me,
the waves that rock me,
the sun that draws me.

You are the beginning and the end of my
    longing,
my place of peace,
my heart's restlessness.

Gentle One, Powerful One,
draw me always to yourself.
Let me not be afraid
of the restlessness and desire
that fills me when I gaze into your light.

Increase my longing,
give me your peace,
carry me home.

surrendering

You are a fish swimming in the ocean of God.

Sai Baba

the forest

1. Encountering the Forest

paying attention

The world of life, of spontaneity, the world of dawn and sunset and starlight, the world of soil and sunshine, of meadow and woodland, of hickory and oak and maple and hemlock and pineland forests, of wildlife dwelling around us, of the river and its well-being—all of this some of us are discovering for the first time as the integral community in which we live. Here we experience the reality and the values that evoke in us our deepest moments of reflection, our revelatory experience of the ultimate mystery of things. Here . . . we receive those larger intuitions that lead us to dance and sing, intuitions that activate our imaginative powers in their most creative functions.

Thomas Berry

pondering

When my son Peter was just three, and his sister Christine not yet one, we lived on the edge of a great forest. Harriman State Park stretched for miles to the north and east of our home. On spring evenings, when their mom was working late, we would set out for a hike in the woods. With our Bernese Mountain Dog, Bernie, bounding enthusiastically ahead of us, and with

Christine riding regally in her seat upon my back, Peter and I would talk and sing as we hiked along. He was a tireless walker and delighted in Bernie's rousting out pheasants or surprising a doe and her fawn. One time we met a French Canadian couple, Renée and Laurent, who were walking their wire-haired terrier Bijou. They raved about the children, and we told stories about the antics of our dogs. We called Renée and Laurent, our "forest friends," for although we would often meet them, we never saw them outside of the woods.

I have always loved to walk in the woods, but discovering the forest through my son's eyes that spring gave me a new sense of it. It was a magical, living place for him, where dogs and people, deer and pheasants, towering trees and rushing brooks all existed in harmony. He was at home there, discovering himself with innocence and simplicity as a part of a world of life and spontaneity. And I was discovering myself anew as well, in a way that would not have been possible were it not for his joy. I too was recognizing that I was a part of the life of the forest, that it was not only a place to go to think about my concerns or to resolve my problems, but it was a place to go simply for its own sake. And in that place I experienced a creative energy and fellowship with all of its inhabitants.

Recently we had the chance to visit those woods again. Bernie has been dead a long time now, and we were filled with nostalgia as we walked through the woods and remembered those days. Then up ahead we saw a couple walking toward us with their own Bernese. He was almost identical to our beloved Bernie, with the same wild exuberance and energy. Amazed and delighted, we left the woods that day aware that we are indeed part of a wonderful community of life.

responding

There is a world of life and spontaneity
that exists all around me
apart from my knowledge and awareness.

Its harmony invites me,
its fellowship awaits me,
its mystery beckons me.

It is not remote or too far away,
yet I rush along, heedless of its call.

Yet whenever I return to the forest,
I discover there a timeless presence
whose eternal hand welcomes me.

At peace, I am no longer isolated,
the forest's life envelops me
and gives me back my own.

surrendering

The trees and stone will teach you what you never learn from the masters.

Bernard of Clairvaux

2. Sensing the Forest's Beauty

paying attention

Beyond a fallen tree I noticed a small clearing covered with leaves, dimly lit and inviting. . . . I stood leaning against the fallen tree and remained quiet.

I don't know how long I waited, getting used to the untroubled sounds of the trees and distant birds, the occasional movement of chipmunks in the leaves. But suddenly I heard something in the brush to my right. The sound was different from the others, heavier. I knew it was made by something more conscious than the other creatures around. I felt not only its weight, but also its consciousness—its frightening likeness to myself. A person, I thought, or a dog. Then I saw it. . . . It was a deer, a young doe, I think.

Staying perfectly still, I breathed as lightly as possible, my warm breath nevertheless smoking around my face in the cold air. Gradually, the deer made its way into the clearing where I had been waiting . . . suddenly she saw me. She stopped fast, stamping her right front hoof, moving her head up and down, then side to side, studying me intently. She wagged her white tail fiercely and seemed to gaze through me with those large, dark eyes. For a moment she jumped back into the brush, but I waited, and soon she came back out, eyeing me carefully but walking on in the direction she had been heading. Down the slope to water no doubt. I watched until she disappeared.

Belden Lane

⌒pondering

Moments of encounter like this one described by Belden Lane are rare indeed, as rare perhaps between us humans as between ourselves and the animals. We all share a natural defensiveness that makes us wary of one another, that keeps us from truly seeing each other.

An appreciation of the beauty in the other begins with an awareness of what Lane describes here as the other's "frightening likeness" to myself. The security of my isolation is disrupted by the presence of another consciousness. When we look into another's eyes, we recognize the disarming similarities between us, but also the unfamiliar, the strange.

The fragile beauty of such a moment of encounter is grasped not in the first moment of contact, but when Lane is able to let down his guard and simply be in the presence of this other life. His being stronger, and the doe no threat, made it an easy matter for him. But the wild deer would have none of this, moving quickly, warily away. This discovery of beauty came as an unexpected gift. Is there a way of being in the forest that allows me to discover a similar beauty? What risk might be involved opening myself to such a revelation? What might I lose in this process? What might I gain?

Just beyond the initial recognition of similarity and difference, a discovery of beauty awaits us.

responding

Quiet my chipmunk mind,
focus my darting heart,
open wide my eyes.

Teach me to wait silently,
untroubled and without fear,
to be a part of the whole.

Grant me but a glimpse
of the disarming similarities
and the frightening differences.

And in those large dark eyes
let me see myself more clearly,
so like and unlike the forest's beauty.

surrendering

In stillness my soul awaits you.

Psalm 62

3. The Comfort of the Forest

✐paying attention

The dark boughs reach out above me and encircle me like arms. I feel the assurance of being recognized, as if something powerful and protective is aware of my presence, looks in another direction, but always has me in the corner of its eye. I am cautious and self-protective here, as anywhere, yet I believe that a covenant of mutual regard binds me together with the forest. We share in a common nurturing. Each of us serves as an amulet to protect the other from inordinate harm. I am never alone in this wild forest, this forest of elders, this forest of eyes.

Richard Nelson

✐pondering

One day, as I walked through those same Harriman woods, along a fast moving stream called Stony Brook, I noticed a massive tree trunk bridging the banks. Walking to its midpoint, I lay down upon it and gazed upward. My fingers found a hold on its smooth weathered surface, keeping me balanced, my spine resting easily on its curve. Beneath me the cold rushing water, above me a canopy of glimmering leaves against a deep blue sky.

As I rested there I sensed, encircling me, the presence of all those who love me, the living and the dead. Cradled by the forest, lulled by the rhythm of the stream, warmed by the dappled sunlight, I was comforted and covenanted in a bond of mutual regard with them, and with the life around me. Joined together, we were all caught up in the powerful, protective gaze of Love.

responding

Hold me in the corner of your eye
watchful and protective, yet freeing.

Say that you know me
and my need for comfort and assurance.

Cradle me in your arms
encircling the present and the future.

For we are far from strangers you and I,
bound in a covenant of mutual regard,
ringed around in a circle of love.

surrendering

God is a circle whose circumference is here and whose center is everywhere.

Hindu scripture

4. Standing in Awe

After one has seen pines six feet in diameter bending like grasses before a mountain gale, and ever and anon some giant falling with a crash that shakes the hills, it seems astonishing that any, save the lowest thickest trees, could ever have found a period sufficiently stormless to establish themselves; or, once established, that they should not, sooner or later, have been blown down. But then the storm is over, and we behold the forests tranquil again, towering fresh and unscathed in erect majesty, and consider what centuries of storms have fallen upon them since they were first planted—hail, to break the tender seedlings; lightning, to scorch and shatter; snow, winds, and avalanches, to crush and overwhelm—while the manifest result of all this wild storm-culture is the glorious perfection we behold; then faith in Nature's forestry is established, and we cease to deplore the violence of her most destructive gales, or of any other storm implement whatsoever.

John Muir

Awalk in the woods along the bank of the St. Joseph River reminded me of what an unkempt place the forest is. In this rare stretch of old growth forest in park land spanning Indiana and Michigan, one finds readily the "wild storm-culture" John Muir described. A huge oak stands snapped at midpoint, the remains of its crown scattered like rubble about it. The once stately tree clings to life. The remains of decaying logs crisscross a field of milky white trillium flowers like a deranged sampler. Below them a thick mat of last year's leaves blankets the rich loam of the river's shore.

It strikes me that it's not at all the way I would have arranged it. No one clears away the debris to let the beauty of the flowers show, no one takes down the ruined trunk and plants a new sapling, no one straightens up nature's mess. This is not a garden, it's a forest. Gardens inspire admiration for the way the gardener has crafted and arranged the natural beauty of flowers, shrubs, and trees. A forest inspires something else again—awe. Amidst the remnants of the storm's chaos, beauty blooms. The broken and the shattered stand side by side with the enduring and the strong.

Its perfection is not in symmetry. Rather, it strikes a chord with dissonant notes. It is an acquired taste.

responding

I stand in awe of nature's forestry,
all the more of her shaping my heart
not with a gardener's careful cultivation,
but with a seemingly careless display,
with a rugged and rough touch.

Yet never absent nor neglectful,
always allowing the grotesque and the delicate
to sit side by side,
always drawing out of chaos
with the awesome power of life.

surrendering

We all continually move on the edges of eternity.

Ansel Adams

paying attention

Woods are not like other spaces. To begin with, they are cubic. Their trees surround you, loom over you, press in from all sides. Woods choke off views and leave you muddled and without bearings. They make you feel small and confused and vulnerable, like a small child lost in a crowd of strange legs. Stand in a desert or prairie and you know you are in a big space. Stand in a woods and you only sense it. They are a vast featureless nowhere. And they are alive.

So woods are spooky. . . . There is something innately sinister about them, some ineffable thing that makes you sense an atmosphere of pregnant doom with every step and leaves you profoundly aware that you are out of your element and ought to keep your ears pricked. Though you tell yourself it's preposterous, you can't quite shake the feeling that you are being watched. . . . Every sudden noise—the crack of a falling limb, the crash of a bolting deer—makes you spin in alarm and stifle a plea for mercy.

Bill Bryson

Hansel and Gretel. Goldilocks. Little Red Riding Hood. Many of our childhoods were filled with these stories, stories in which the forest played as much a part as any bear, wolf, or witch. That's why the spookiness of the woods which Bill Bryson describes resonates with our imaginations even today. Fairy tales such as these arose in medieval Europe at a time when the forest was always nearby, a dangerous foreboding place.

Very few of us have such an experience of the forest today. We would have to travel some distance to find ourselves in a forest of genuine magnitude, a place where one could get truly lost. Nevertheless, we can quite easily imagine the paralyzing fear that being lost in a forest would cause us when we reflect on moments in life when we have lost our way. We become disoriented, we have a sense of helplessness, and we are afraid. We don't know which way to turn. Thus it is that the experience of being lost in the woods has become a metaphor for the psychological and spiritual experience of being lost. "Midway on the journey of life I awoke to find myself alone and lost in a dark wood, having wandered from the straight path," Dante wrote.

What we lose in the woods is our sense of direction, and we are powerless without it. Regaining that sense requires us to look in two directions: inward and outward. We look within to retrace our steps, to rediscover how we came to be in this place. Perhaps we can remember where we went off course and find our way back onto the path. Yet we must take care to avoid the snares of regret and self-blame that will, should we dwell overly on them, bind us to the past. Having turned inward, we can begin to find reasons to be hopeful. Then we look outward to try to get our bearings, "to see the forest for the trees." As we remember our purpose and direction, we can begin to find our way.

Hansel and Gretel, Goldilocks, and Little Red Riding Hood all used their wits to find their way safely out of the forest. Dante had the spiritual guidance of Beatrice. We need both wit and wisdom if we are to find our way.

responding

In the landscape of my life
there are forests I try to avoid,
places in my past (and in my present)
I do not like to go.

Still I lose my way in the tangle
of difficult and confusing relationships,
resentments, hurts, and unfinished business.
I don't know how to get back on the path.

"This again," I whine,
realizing I've wandered off course
into muddy terrain I promised to avoid
having failed to mark the trail.

Mired in self-pity
I stand there confused,
abandoned, and forsaken,
wallowing in my sorrow.

You who are the compass of my life,
ease my fears of being powerless,
help me remember I'm not alone,
guide my steps one at a time.

surrendering

L et yourself go and let God be in you.

Meister Eckhart

6. The Call of the Forest

paying attention

I went to the woods because I wished to live deliberately, to front only the essential facts of life, and see if I could not learn what it had to teach, and not, when I came to die, discover that I had not lived. I did not wish to live what was not life, living is so dear; nor did I wish to practice resignation, unless it was quite necessary. I wanted to live deep and suck out all the marrow of life, to live so sturdily and Spartan-like as to put to rout all that was not life, to cut a broad swath and shave close, to drive life into a corner, and reduce it to its lowest terms, and, if it proved to be mean, why then to get the whole and genuine meanness of it, and publish its meanness to the world; or if it were sublime, to know it by experience, and be able to give a true account of it in my next excursion.

Henry David Thoreau

pondering

To live deliberately; to live an examined life, consciously, "mindfully" as the Buddhists would say; to live each day to the fullest, seeing the essence of life in each moment and not arriving at a point where the life I have lived is not really a life—this is why Thoreau went to the woods, this is the call I hear from them.

"Living is so dear," Thoreau says, so he went to the woods to deepen his appreciation for what is most authentic and real, for the precious quality of life that is always revealing itself in momentary glimpses and then passing away. The woods served as an antidote for all that was distracting and false in the ordinary course of things.

His deliberate life in the woods was not a matter of passive stillness. He built a cabin, planted a field, wrote, studied, entertained visitors, and went frequently to town. "I wanted to suck out all the marrow of life . . . to live Spartan-like." While he was certainly no hermit, he had an ascetic energy in him which drove him to search out the deepest meaning of things.

Ralph Waldo Emerson once described his friend Thoreau in this way: "He knew but one secret, which was to do but one thing at a time." This is the Thoreau who was aware of the significance of each moment, seeking a higher level of consciousness, discovering connections between himself, his companions, and nature. He has something to learn from the woods themselves, and he listens attentively.

If I am to hear the call of the forest and discover what it has to say to me, I must let go of the desire, the need to master life, the tendency to view the forest merely as a place where I can drive life into a corner. I must learn from the forest that life is a complex web of birth, growth, death, and rebirth. As each thing in the forest lives only as it is meant to do, so must I learn to heed the many dimensions of who I am, honoring each and responding to each in concert with all the rest. I must learn to do "but one thing at a time."

responding

The spider simply weaves its web
without vanity or striving.
Finishing in due course,
then it waits.

Each forest creature does the same,
follows its way without resistance or denial,
being simply what it is,
living its unexamined life.

What can I learn from those "thoughtless"
    creatures
about reflection and self-awareness?
They are who they are
without concern or abstraction.

The forest calls me to discover who I am,
to cultivate an inner and outer awareness,
to be keenly aware of the world around me,
and the spirit within me.

You who gave the spider such a single heart,
attune my soul to live deliberately, carefully,
         naturally,
to find a balance between striving and waiting,
between resistance and resignation.

Teach me to do one thing at a time.

surrendering

Simplify, simplify, simplify.

Henry David Thoreau

7. Moving in the Forest's Rhythm

Here lies an old log, long fallen, long rotted, crumbling to the dark soil it came from. . . . No stump is visible; the limbs are long gone, the bark vanished. Only this bulk or core of a once-tree yet remains. It was a tree, to be sure, unknown years ago, wind-wrecked or fallen from disease; now it lies and rots its long way to disappearance. *Anicca,* impermanent. It was a tree, of a certain species, and now we call it a rotten log. At what point did the one term fail and the other apply? From tree to log to mealy dust there occurs a continual changing, a gliding of form into form that we follow imprecisely with language. The stages we see and try to express in language do not exist outside of our imagination, because change never ceases, never pauses to draw a line and give us notice.

Bhikkhu Nyanasobhano

pondering

The rhythm of the forest is the rhythm of change. The end of the tree is part of a process that has been going on since life began. And it will continue until life comes to an end. Whether I look at the seed which falls to the ground and sprouts to life, at the cycle of the seasons, or at the disappearance of a stump, I see but a moment's glimpse in a constant process of change. Change never ceases.

Almost nine years ago, when my family first moved into our house, there was a dying tree in the yard. Tall and slender, the tree was precariously close to the house, and on the windward side. One day a stranger in overalls carrying a chain saw knocked at the door. He had observed the tree and offered to cut it. We agreed on a price and the tree was soon felled, leaving only the stump, about eighteen inches high.

When spring came, my daughter Sarah was born. That summer some potted impatiens bloomed on the stump. Then we put a squirrel feeder on it. When Sarah grew she would play on it, sometimes sitting, sometimes jumping off it. But as the years passed, she took no particular interest in it. I alone was watching.

As I cleaned up in the yard early this spring I noticed the stump was falling apart. When I laid my hand on it, it crumbled. A few light swings of the ax and it was gone. In April, Sarah turned eight, full of energy, laughter, and promise.

"Nothing gold can stay," Robert Frost once wrote about the birch leaves in fall. But leaves have many colors in their brief lives and all are beautiful. The stump was pleasing as it made its way to dust, counting the years of Sarah's childhood. And Sarah is always a new and surprising gift as she grows each day.

Anicca. Impermanent. Some say change is good, some say not. But since there is no choice about it, I choose to embrace change. If I resist, I will miss the new opportunities it offers and drain myself fighting it. Though accepting it is sometimes painful, in the midst of the pain I find glimpses of hope.

responding

Are you, O maker of the cosmos,
creator of the atom,
are you without change?

Do you stand aloof, uninvolved
in the ever expanding universe
where no matter is static?

Or is your eternal quality
the energy of change?
Is your power in your presence?

In my losing, is it not you I find?
In my dying, do you not bring me to birth?
In my dissolution, do you not remake me?

O ever changing love,
O eternal energy of presence,
in you all things pass away,
in you all things arise anew.

surrendering

A resolute attention to the course of things . . . strikes off the sparks of insight that light our darkness.

Bhikkhu Nyanasobhano

8. Carrying the Forest Within You

paying attention

I wonder what it would be like to go into a forest where nothing had a name. If there were no word for tree stumps, would they sink into the duff? It's possible: After all, earth without form is void. And if we started over, giving names, would any fact about the forest compel us to name the same units? Would we label trees? Or instead would we find a name for the unity of roots and soil and microorganisms? Or would we label only the gross of light on leaves and the shapes of shadows on the bark? How would we act in a forest if there were no names for anything smaller than an ecosystem? How could we walk, if there were no way to talk about anything larger than a cell?

Kathleen Dean Moore

pondering

What of the forest do I carry within me? Images, sounds, smells, feelings—of many times, of many places: mountain laurels in bloom as I run along a familiar path; a startled deer bolting ahead of me; the pungent smell of pine and the hot sun on my back; the pain in my thighs as I struggle up yet another hill; snow piled thick on evergreen boughs against a deep blue sky; the staccato sound of the woodpecker rapping on a tree trunk; the familiar song of the cardinal at dawn.

My words fall short, suggesting only vaguely the forest's lush form. Each image is but a marker of a moment in my life, a symbol of a complex set of experiences, emotions, beliefs, and dreams. Together they form the ecology of my soul, an ever growing, ever changing web of life. The forest world, teeming with life, bursting with energy, yet simultaneously dissolving into dust, is a mirror of my soul. For it too is a mysterious deep, seemingly endless wood.

I seek to name its thickets and clearings, its streams and its glens, yet with each naming a boundary wall is built, a territory is carved out. With each thing that is understood, something is set aside, as if it did not belong. For what little is known, more is unknown.

Yet how can I trace a path through my life if there is no way to name the woods I traverse? With all that is learned, let me hold in my memory the sense of the whole, of that which cannot be named. Let me carry the forest within me.

responding

I carry you within me,
just as you carry me.
You who console and comfort,
inspire and instruct,
shelter and shape my soul.

More than a refuge,
you are a complex community
living in me as I live in you.
If I look I will see you.
If I listen I will hear.

You call me to live.
You call me home.
I want to answer.

surrendering

Words are the last resort for what lies within.

Rainer Maria Rilke

the desert

1. Encountering the Desert

paying attention

You must come [to the desert] with no intentions of discovery. You must overhear things, as though you'd come to a small and desolate town and paused by an open window. . . . You have to proceed almost by accident.

Barry Lopez

pondering

What attitude is necessary to learn from the desert? Lopez reminds those of us who come to the desert looking for some kind of experience that we will probably go away empty. Such a warning goes against our grain.

We come to the desert expecting to wait, but we are often unprepared for the depth of the waiting involved. When the desert does not offer up its secrets, we go away angry and tell the story of our fruitless search. Then, in the telling, we recognize something we think we may have missed—perhaps there is another way in. And so we return. But still, there is no answer. The desert chides us, "You can't get at it this way."

One must simply be there, "with no intentions of discovery." When we are trying to learn from the desert, there is nothing to be gained. But when we've given up the idea of getting something out of a desert sojourn, we may accidentally discover that without knowing it, we've been changed. We don't take something from it, but it changes us. Lopez concludes his reflection with these words: "One morning I noticed my hands had begun to crack and turn to dust."

responding

I sit and wait,
trying not to try,
wanting not to want.
I have no intention of discovery,
I have not set my heart on gain,
and yet. . . .

My steps are not accidental,
my hands are still flesh.
Do I truly want to remember
that I am made of dust?

surrendering

In the desert the most urgent thing is to wait.

Alessandro Ponzato

2. Sensing the Desert's Beauty

paying attention

At last, Dahoum drew me. "Come and smell the sweetest scent of all," and we went to the main lodging, to the gaping window sockets of its eastern face, and there drank with open mouths of the effortless empty, eddyless wind of the desert, throbbing past.

T. E. Lawrence

pondering

Because the desert overwhelms some of our senses, there is a danger that those senses which are not so dramatically affected will fail to function. But if we are to sense the desert's beauty, we must learn to take it in through those senses which are not so obviously captured by it. The brightness of the sun blinds our eyes. The heat of the sand burns our feet. But what about our sense of smell, our hearing, our taste buds? What does the desert smell like? How does it taste? What melody does it sing to us?

In this brief vignette, T. E. Lawrence and his young protégé Dahoum inhale the desert's sweetness, they drink of its unceasing wind. Young Dahoum has lived his whole life in the desert and knows it well. Lawrence is older, yet he is still learning the subtleties of desert existence. Though usually the mentor, he is the one in need of guidance here.

The beauty of the desert is illusive. To discover it we must proceed artfully, relying not on the obvious, but the unexpected, proceeding not from our strengths, but daring to approach it with a sense of our vulnerability. The desert purifies our senses, refining our ability to perceive what is beautiful.

The experience of discovering beauty in the desert has taught me how to be receptive to the unexpected manifestations of beauty in unusual places. There are the desert places within me, and there are the desert places that life leads me to—places of anxiety, frustration, or exhaustion, places like hospital rooms, for example. In the places I frequent, it is hard not to follow the lead of my dominant sense and to be swept away by the emotions which flow from it. The smell of sickness, for example, is frightening. . . . But if I can cultivate my vision to see the fear in my sick friend's eyes, we can connect in our fear. If I can place my hand on his shoulder, I can break the isolation that grips us both.

The desert is beautiful. If I know that, it is not a question of creating something that is not there, but of discovering how to be receptive to the illusive, hidden beauty.

The blazing sun is too much for my eyes,
my feet are beginning to burn through my
    shoes.
I want to flee, to get away quickly.

How can I stay here?
What must I do to be in this place
without being overwhelmed?

Help me find a place where I can begin
to remember that there is a hidden beauty
in the desert's apparent harshness.

Teach me to be receptive to beauty
and to search it out
knowing it is there.

surrendering

The desert is the Garden of Allah.

Algerian saying

3. The Comfort of the Desert

paying attention

Rain loomed over him. It hung over the northeast slopes of Black Mesa like a wall—illuminated to light gray now and then by sheet lightning. The smell of it came through the pickup vents mixed with the smell of dust. In Chee's desert trained nostrils, it was heady perfume—the smell of good grazing, easy water, heavy crops of piñon nuts. The smell of good times, the smell of Sky Father blessing Mother Earth.

Tony Hillerman

pondering

For Jim Chee, the younger of the two Navajo tribal police officers in Tony Hillerman's mystery novels about life on the reservation, just the smell of the approaching rain is enough to evoke an array of images, all expressions of the blessing that the rain bestows. Though not a Navajo himself, Hillerman understands well the Navajo concept of *hozro*, living in harmony with one's environment. Chee, who is both a detective and an aspiring shaman, seeks above all to live in such harmony with his desert surroundings.

For Chee, the rain does indeed bring comfort in the desert's dryness; its ozone-laden smell promises good grazing, easy water, and a rich harvest. Because he has learned to live through the dry times, he appreciates the rain. And even in the desert, the rain eventually comes.

But is the comfort of the desert discovered only when it ceases to be desert, when the rains at last come? Relief is not the same thing as comfort. Is there such a thing as comfort in the midst of the desert? Jim Chee would no doubt say yes, that the comfort is in the *hozro*, in achieving harmony. The comfort of the desert comes from knowing it deeply, perceiving its hidden beauty, learning its rhythms and cycles. This is not the easy comfort of a spring morning in the forest, or a summer afternoon by the shore. It is a comfort that grows gradually as one learns to be at home in the desert, living carefully on what it provides, respecting those creatures who also know how to live there.

When such harmony has been learned, the deeper meaning of the desert's blessings can be appreciated—its sunsets, its star-strewn skies, and its rarest gift, rain.

responding

O Desert One,
whose face is the sand's warmth and
    roughness,
whose breath is the hot wind
    that stirs in the evening,
whose touch sears like the sun,
keep me in your sight,
tame my desire to flee from your gaze.
Teach me your ways, O Desert One.
Let me hear you in the silence.
Let me see you in the emptiness.
Let me touch you in this desert earth.
May I learn to strive always for *hozro*,
and to live in harmony with you.

surrendering

The desert contains every gift within itself.

Carlo Carretto

4. Standing in Awe

How often have I known that living picture of the desert night of the Sahara!

How often, lying wrapped in a blanket of sand, have I passed hour after hour gazing at the starry dome ceaselessly speaking to me, questioning me, helping me find my bearings in the dark!

Why do we live?

Why do things come to be?

Why do I plod along like a wandering shepherd?

Why this vast silence?

Why do the stars look down as though indifferent to our suffering?

Withal, one thing is certain: this light, the sign of the truth we seek and the means by which we catch a glimpse of it, has not got its roots on earth.

Light comes from up there. From something stretching above me, something transcending me, something preceding me.

Carlo Carretto

The sky at night, the unrelenting sun by day, the horizon that never seems to come closer, the power of a storm—there are so many ways that the desert can leave us awestruck. Carlo Carretto knew this well. He gave up a promising career as an educator in post-War Italy to join a religious community dedicated to living a simple life in the midst of the poor. Thus he found himself in an obscure Tuareg village in the Sahara. There, as he struggled to understand the mystery at the heart of the world and in the depths of himself, he frequently found himself awestruck by the Sahara.

To be in awe is to fall silent. The Bible, as well as other sacred sources, often relates that a person who has come into contact with God has been struck dumb. Confronted with the awe of a desert sky at night, we too may fall silent. But this silence often moves quickly to questioning. As we recognize our smallness before the desert sky at night, we can get our bearings. To find our way, we begin to ask questions. Like Carretto, we wonder why things are the way they are, how it is that we are here in this place at this moment, awestruck by this beauty and power.

But soon we find ourselves no longer questioning, but being questioned. The desert begins to speak to us, to question us. The desert questions us, as God questioned Job: "Where were you when I laid the foundation of the earth? Tell me, if you have understanding. Who determined its measurements—surely you know" (Job 38:4).

Before such majesty we fall silent again, not with the first silence, a silence of astonishment. Now we are silent with a humble silence, a contemplative silence that recognizes that what we are seeing is more than we can comprehend, and that somehow, we are a part of this mystery. As Carretto said, we are part of something transcending us, something preceding us.

responding

How often I place myself at the center.
When I see the power, the beauty, the majesty
    of nature
I am struck with awe and wonder,
I marvel that it is all here for me.

Yet the marvel is not that it is here for me,
putting on a cosmic show to dazzle me.
Rather, the marvel is that I am a part of it,
living and breathing with it.

The divine reality encompasses me,
holding me in the fold of its garment
as it stretches out its arm
with a galactic sweep.

O hidden heart of the cosmos,
whose pulse beats within me,
teach me to be silent before your majesty,
hold me secure in the shadow of your wing.

surrendering

The desert is where God is and man is not.

Ibn Kaldoun'

paying attention

"I will tell you something about the Sahara," he finally says, pulling off his gold-rimmed glasses to wipe them clean. "The desert is very simple to survive in. You must only admit there is something on earth larger than you . . . the wind . . . the dryness . . . the distance . . . the Sahara. You accept that and everything is fine. The desert will provide. *Inshallah.* If you do not, the desert will break you. Admit your weakness to the Sahara's face, and all is fine."

Nouhou Agah

pondering

There is something on earth larger than me. In the desert, this fact is inescapable. The wind, the dryness, the distance confront me with my limits, my mortality. Even those things smaller than me, be they plant or animal, rate seemingly hostile—sharp, piercing, poisonous. I alone stand out as the one not adapted to this place. I am the one who does not know how to survive.

The desert has no patience with denial of this or any other realities. It demands my admission of powerlessness. Whatever technology I may have at my disposal is but a thin veil before the desert's power. It is no substitute for respect, for deference.

"Admit your weakness, and all is fine." How is it fine? Such an admission does not make us equals. It does not make the desert benevolent. It does not make it easy to find my way, to survive. But the fact of my weakness is the truth. It is not an easy truth, but it is true.

I am smaller. I am powerless. And in this truth there is a freedom. When I know the terms of our engagement, my relationship with the desert changes. The mirage of control disappears. Then I seek to coexist, to live in reverence. Then the desert will provide. *Inshallah.*

responding

Inshallah, God willing.
If Allah wills it, it will be so.

You who hold the Sahara in your hand,
whose skin is as supple as the shifting sands,
it is you whose willingness is greater than my
     will.

May the wind of your constancy
erode the stoniness of my heart.
May the dryness of your fidelity
preserve me in readiness.

May the distance of your touch
teach me to stay awake.

Hold me in your willingness,
secure me in your hand.
Let me not run from my powerlessness
or get lost in my will.

If you will it,
it will be so.

surrendering

The desert loves to strip bare.

Jerome

6. The Call of the Desert

paying attention

For over three months I had labored across the Sahara, and there had been few moments when I had experienced the magnetism of the desert to which so many people before me had succumbed. But now, in the utmost isolation, I began at last to understand its attraction. It was the awful scale of the thing, the suggestion of virginity, the fusion of pure elements from the heavens above and the earth beneath which were untrammeled and untouched by anything contrived by any human being.

Geoffrey Moorhouse

pondering

The call of the desert is a call to clarity, to simplicity. In the religions of the West, it has always been so. Moses, Jesus, and Mohammed all heard the desert's call as a summons to discover their identity, to clarify their purpose, to encounter the Holy One. They were grasped by a desert presence. The desert itself presented a call that could not be ignored, and in its expanse they found the one who called them.

Such a sharply delineated sense of purpose stands in stark contrast to the ordinary course of our lives. We are not easily grasped by a desert presence. Like the journalist Geoffrey Moorhouse, who traveled for three months in the Sahara before he experienced its magnetism, we find ourselves in the midst of a desert landscape without any sense of clarity or purpose.

The initial excitement of a call to a relationship, to a job, to some particular commitment fades, and we find ourselves well along the road without any clear sense of who we are or why we are doing what we do. It was, Moorhouse wrote, "in the utmost desolation" that he began to sense the attraction of the desert. Perhaps we too must reach a point of no return, where our only option is to follow the path that we are on, before we can rediscover the original power of its call to us.

It was, for Moorhouse, in grasping "the awful scale of the thing" that he began to sense the purity of the desert, its mystical union of heaven and earth. The call of the desert, for we who live apart from its stark beauty, is an invitation to cultivate a sense of clarity and simplicity in our lives. As we attempt to look on life from these perspectives we may, at times, discover the original magnetism that led us to set out on the way.

responding

What is this desert road I travel
and how did I come to be on it?
It wasn't a desert way when I first set out

and I do not know when it changed,
but now it has become one.
I never left the path
but I seem to have lost my way
and forgotten why I set out.

I've come too far to return.
I do not know any other way to go.
At this point of utmost isolation
I call to you.
Open my eyes to see again
the vision that first impelled me.
Simplify my heart to rediscover
the magnetism of your call.

As I begin again
let me practice simplicity.
As I continue on this path,
renew my sense of purpose.
Then I will be captured anew
by the simple beauty of this desert.
I will be drawn willingly
into its deepest dimensions.

surrendering

My soul longs for you,
like a dry weary land without water.

Psalm 63

7. Moving in the Desert's Rhythm

❦ *paying attention*

The desert assigns its own slow rhythm—a rhythm from beyond silence, from beyond life—to the smallest gesture, the most insignificant word.

In the desert one becomes other: the one who knows the weight of the sky and the thirst of the earth; the one who has learned to take account of his own solitude. Far from excluding us, the desert envelopes us. We become the immensity of sand. . . .

Edmund Jabès

❦ *pondering*

On the most accessible level, the rhythm of the desert is the rhythm of day and night. Relentless sun and unfathomable stars, blinding heat and blessed coolness. Then there is the rhythm of the seasons, long months of dryness interrupted by a brief season of rain. But the poet Edmund Jabès seems to speak here of a different type of rhythm, slower than day and night, slower even than the seasons. It is a rhythm that is discovered only by one who ventures into a relationship with the desert.

In such a relationship, we do not dictate the times or the seasons; the desert assigns its own slow rhythm. Beyond silence, beyond life, it is the rhythm of a limitless thirst, of an endless desire. In this stark landscape of contrasts, each gesture, each word has eternal implications.

The rhythm of the desert is the rhythm of absorption. "In the desert one becomes other." As we come to know the desert we realize the expanse of our solitude. As water evaporates into sky, so we are absorbed, enveloped by the desert. The apparent contrasts of the desert are broken down. Day and night, rain and sun, life and death no longer stand as opposites; they are all consumed by the desert, according to its own slow rhythm. There is only the sand, and we too are absorbed into the immensity of the sand.

responding

I am more at ease with predictable rhythms:
day and night, rainy and dry.
Though beyond my control,
I am secure in the knowledge
that one follows the other.

There are no easy rhythms to be found
in the weight of the sky, the thirst of the earth,
the expanse of my solitude.
These frighten me.
What becomes of the raindrop in the desert?

Who are you
beyond silence, beyond life,
who absorbs and envelopes me?
And what will I be
if I become the immensity of sand?

surrendering

We are saved in the end by the things that
ignore us.

Andrew Harvey

8. Carrying the Desert Within You

paying attention

Earth. Rock. Desert. I am walking barefoot on the sandstone, flesh responding to flesh. It is hot, so hot the rock threatens to burn through the callused soles of my feet. I must quicken my pace, paying attention to where I step.

For as far as I can see, the canyon country of southern Utah extends in all directions. No compass can orient me here, only a pledge to love and walk the terrifying distances before me. What I fear and desire most in this world is passion. I fear it because it promises to be spontaneous, out of my control, unnamed, beyond my reasonable self. I desire it because passion has color, like the landscape before me. It is not pale. It is not neutral. It reveals the backside of the heart.

Terry Tempest Williams

pondering

The desert is disorienting. Whether it is the shifting sands of the Sahara or the wild complexity of Utah's canyon country, it is hard to find one's way. We must pay attention, watch every step, not lose what fragile bearings we may have. The burning heat of the sand on our feet makes us move quickly and decisively.

Life is disorienting. When we come to recognize the harsh desert landscape as the terrain of our hearts, we realize that the orientation we seek can only come from within. As the desert becomes part of us, we have only our pledge of fidelity to guide us. Fidelity requires loving. In the concrete reality of the here and now, it calls for courage, the willingness to move forward, despite the terrifying distances before us.

Fidelity, if it is to be real and alive, must be passionate. One cannot be passively faithful. Passion is dangerous, it is risky, not so easy to predict or control. Yet to live passionately is to live without pretense, vulnerably. When we live this way, we explore not only the shallow realms of our hearts, but those desires that call to us from the depths, from the back side.

To live passionately is to remember that the desert is always within us. It is to move forward without hesitation, in love, despite our fears— seeking always to be faithful.

responding

You who are the compass of my heart,
teach me to love and to walk despite my fears,
help me to learn what it is to be faithful.

You who lurk behind my longing,
increase my desire, cast out my fears,
let me become passionate as you are.

Let me not run from the desert
but carry it within me,
and be made whole, be made one, in its light.

Earth. Rock. Desert.
Body. Soul. Spirit.
Not three, but one.

surrendering

The labyrinths time creates vanish.
(The only thing left is the desert.)

Federico García Lorca

the river

1. Encountering the River

How he loved this river, how it enchanted him, how grateful he was to it! In his heart he heard the newly awakened voice speak, and it said to him: "Love this river, stay by it, learn from it." Yes, he wanted to learn from it. It seemed to him that whoever understood this river and its secrets, would understand much more, many secrets, all secrets.

But today he only saw one of the river's secrets, one that gripped his soul. He saw that the water continually flowed and flowed and yet it was always there; it was always the same and yet every moment it was new. Who could understand, conceive this?

Hermann Hesse

pondering

For almost three years, when we were first married, my wife and I lived on the shore of the Hudson River. That's not the way most people would describe life in Manhattan, but to me, being near the river was one of the best things about where we lived. I clung to the connection to the natural world that it provided. In the midst of traffic, noise, and crime it was something of a lifeline.

We lived at the northern tip of Manhattan Island, where the Harlem River connects with the Hudson. Because of the fierce currents at the confluence, the early Dutch settlers named it *Spuyten Duyvil,* meaning "the spite of the devil." I would often walk the path through Isham Park up the hill to get a view of the river and the striking palisades on the New Jersey side. It is the last wooded area in Manhattan. One can walk over a mile through the woods down to Fort Tryon Park where The Cloisters are.

While the Hudson is a far cry from the Ganges, I shared Siddhartha's longing that Hermann Hesse describes. I too wanted to stay by the river, to learn its secrets. It offered me a refuge from city life, but it connected me to the city as well. Along the path I met people of all ages, people of many religions and ethnic backgrounds. As I passed through the park, Dominicans played baseball, yuppies played tennis, Colombians played soccer, and Irish mothers watched their children on the swings.

It was an immersion into history as well. At the base of a hill was a marker of dubious accuracy noting the spot where the Dutch bought Manhattan from the Native Americans. From a personal perspective, when I would look at the river I would sometimes think of Ellis Island, just a few miles downstream, where my grandparents landed on their arrival from Ireland. I would think of how my more distant ancestors from Germany must have disembarked on its shores. As I gazed across the river I would recall the excursions of my childhood, by boat and by car, up the river to Bear Mountain for a picnic.

The endless flow of people, the endless flow of time, the endless flow of the river. Walking through the park on its shore or along the trail through the woods above it, I would ask myself, "Who am I in the midst of it all?"

responding

What are your secrets, O River?
What can you teach me?

I'm afraid I can't stay very long,
I have but this moment . . . this hour.
I do want to learn from you though,
something to take away with me,
some insight to carry me until we meet again.

But you do not yield up your secrets so easily.
So perhaps I can steal another's wisdom . . .
indeed you are changeless, yet ever changing;
always stable, but always flowing;
ever ancient, ever new.

But your secrets are not gained so cheaply, I
      fear.
You do not give yourself to passersby,
but only to those who love you.

Let me learn to love you.
Let me return to you and sit on your bank.
Let me feel you as you flow through me.

Teach me to love you
not for what you give me,
but for yourself.

surrendering

Too late have I loved thee, O Beauty ever
ancient, ever new.

Augustine of Hippo

paying attention

It began, the way it often does on these rivers, when the August sun left the water, the last of the day's bowowing, beer and solar powered rafters passed out of sight, and the daylong breeze inexplicably died. The countless pines ceased their ceaseless *huuuuing*. Deer, seemingly from nowhere, suddenly grazed in the center of every meadow. The sky slipped out of its workaday blue and began trying on the entire evening wardrobe—the lavender, the pink, the pumpkin, even the teal. The river matched it gown for gown, adding warps, wefts and sheens the sky could only dream of. The herons who'd flupped upriver that morning coasted even more slowly back down. The bald eagles who'd coasted down river labored back up. The air—not the sky, but the air itself—turned blue. The day's darting cliff swallows yielded to darting nighthawks and bats. The Blackfoot's became the one voice of the world. Then the river voice, silent pines, blue air, bats and nighthawks merged, just as [Norman] Maclean promised, into one, which oneness became a joy I began to devour in full-bodied, full-hearted gulps.

David James Duncan

The dance of creation goes on, with me or without me, whether I recognize it or not. One moment I am caught up in its movement, weightless in its arms; the next I trip over myself as I return to the everyday world. I long to be the deer who emerges from the wood at dusk, the heron who coasts in the quiet currents of evening. I want to take the place of the sky and be the river's partner, free of care, at peace.

The deer, the heron, the sky are one with the river, but do not know it. I long to be caught up in the river's life as they are and to know it—not just for the moment, but always. I long for perfect harmony.

Is it possible for us who know so much, yet really know so little, to outdo the beauty of the sky as does the river? Perhaps such elusive beauty is but a glimpse of another beauty, even more subtle and difficult to hold. Perhaps the dance of the river is not the only dance.

responding

In the pristine world of unknowing
you are illusive,
yet still I see you, I hear you, I touch you.

But in the world of knowing,
of self-awareness, of longing,
your presence is even more hidden.

Seeing you there
in the heron, in the sky, in the river,
reminds me that you are everywhere,

in words and in silence,
in movement and in stillness,
in holding on and in letting go.

surrendering

Let me see your face, let me hear your voice;
for your voice is sweet and your face is lovely.

Song of Solomon

3. The Comfort of the River

paying attention

[Trudi] looked around. The path winding along the river was empty. So was the meadow that led toward the dike. Quickly, she yanked off her pinafore and the dress with the sailor collar, her stockings and shoes, the white cotton underpants that were buttoned to her undershirt. In the brisk water that still carried the memory of winter, she practiced her swimming as she had imagined. It was amazingly simple—as long as she held the picture of the frog inside her mind. Frogs were at home beneath the surface of the water, and that's where she swam, too, emerging only for deep gulps of air. . . .

Early the following morning she left the house before her father was awake and walked to the river. All that spring she returned there nearly every morning when no one else was near. Staying close to the jetty, she'd streak through the shallow water like a frog, dive to the brown sediment of mud and let it billow around her, wishing her body matched its color so it could camouflage her. Here, the river belonged to her. In the water she felt graceful, weightless even, and when she moved her arms and legs, they felt long.

Ursula Hegi

We speak of memory like a river on which images flow lightly. But real rivers carry memories too, as the novelist Ursula Hegi implies here—memories of seasons, of frogs, of little girls. To submerge oneself in the river, as the child Trudi does, is to participate in the life of the river, to become part of its memory. In it Trudi—a dwarf— becomes graceful, her stunted limbs feel long. She is comforted by the river. In it, she feels at home, whole.

Later, when discovered swimming there by a group of boys who berate her and then molest her, she turns again to the river for comfort. "She wanted to crawl into the river with the shame of having been touched like that, singled out." Picking up stones, she throws them into the river one by one, saying each of the four boys' names as she does so. The river swallows her pain, offers her peace, heals her memory.

What memories does the river hold for me? How does it make me whole? How does it comfort me?

Like a mother holding her child
you comfort me.

As old as the mountains,
as new as the rain,
you are constant and strong,
peaceful and powerful.

Hide me in the stillness of your pools,
nurture me with your abundant life.
Carry me along your gentle flow,
bear me up through your fierce rapids.

Hold me in your memory,
let my heart never forget you.

surrendering

Wherever the river flows it gives life.

The Prophet Ezekiel

4. Standing in Awe

paying attention

I had last seen the Ganges some years before, at Hardiwar. Chloe, my partner, and I had rented a room in the tourist bungalow. One day we were sitting watching the river through the open door. The cleaner emerged from along the corridor and crept into our room with his brown reed brush. He was stooped, older than his years, a sad little man. I was prompted to ask if he had a family. "Yes," he said, and then, after a pause, "but wife sick and children too. No money for medicines, very difficult." He made to start his work and then as if remembering something, he turned and pointed through the door to the river. "But Ma Ganga will take care of us." Without another word, he began sweeping the floor.

I had never heard of anyone speak of a river that way before. For this man, the Ganges was a living presence, a protector, a healer of ills.

Roger Housden

pondering

There is a story in the New Testament about a Roman centurion who approaches Jesus to ask for a healing of his servant. When Jesus agrees to go to the house, the centurion says that is not necessary. Jesus need only give the command and his servant will be healed. To this, Jesus remarks in amazement that nowhere else has he found such faith.

Often, it seems that the most awe-inspiring power is indeed the power of faith. For the aged Hindu man described by Roger Housden in this story, the river inspired such faith. For him, the river was a compassionate presence. In it he recognized the benevolent goodness at the heart of life, even in the midst of his struggle and suffering. Ma Ganga was a spiritual mother to him, and he placed his trust in her.

Such a faith is awe-inspiring. I imagine that the Roman centurion only arrived at such faith because he allowed himself to be touched by the Jewish preacher. When he did, he must have discovered the embers of faith being fanned into a flame within him. So too the Hindu man must have sensed a loving presence in the river, inviting him to trust, to be hopeful when no reasonable hope existed.

Looking at a majestic river is awe-inspiring. But what flows out of that awe within me? It is easy to walk away with a sense of nature's power and beauty. But it takes a deeper sensitivity for me to allow that awe to evolve into trust. This only happens when I recognize that the river is a symbolic presence, through which the goodness and compassion that ever holds the world, holds me too, safely in her arms.

responding

I am blessed in your presence
for you speak softly to me,
inviting me to trust,
offering me hope.

Let me stay by your side
and learn the subtleties of your voice,
as you fill my awe with peace
and draw me beyond passivity.

Say but a word
and my soul will be healed.

surrendering

Go to the earth . . . and ask it for guidance.

Thomas Berry

5. Powerless Before It

✑paying attention

As one watches, there emanates from it . . . an insinuation of darkness, implacability, horror. And the nearer look tends to confirm this. Contained and born in the singular large movements are hundreds of smaller ones: eddies and whirlpools, turnings this way and that, cross currents rushing out from the shores into the channels.

There is something deeply horrifying about it, roused. Not, I think, because it is inhuman, alien to us; some of us at least must feel a kinship to it, or we would not loiter around it for pleasure. The horror must come from our sense that, so long as it remains what it is, it is not subject. To say that it is indifferent would be wrong. That would imply a malevolence, as if it could be aware of us if it wanted to. It is more remote from our concerns than indifference. It is serenely and silently not subject—to us or to anything else except the other natural forces that are also beyond our control. And it is apt to stand for and represent to us all in nature and in the universe that is not subject. That is its horror. We can make use of it. We can ride on its back in boats. But it won't stop to let us go on and off. It is not a passenger train. And if we make a

mistake, or risk ourselves too far to it, why then it
will suffer a little wrinkle on its surface, and go on
as before.

Wendell Berry

pondering

Berry's image of the river brings me up short.
This is not a view in which the river is a
transparent image of the beauty or goodness of the
divine. He recognizes something horrifying in it,
something opaque, something that pays me no
mind. This is not a comforting image of nature.

Contemplating this aspect of the river
challenges me to nuance my awareness of how
nature reflects the divine. This double-edged feeling
of kinship and horror of which Berry speaks is
perhaps the most basic human reaction to an
encounter with the transcendent. One experiences
the divine, as the historian of religions Rudolf Otto
said, as *tremendans et fascinans*. It is awesome,
overpowering, fearsome . . . yet alluring, intriguing,
and wonderful. I am drawn to the river, yet I am
repelled by it. Its raw power can be horrifying.

Who can approach God without fear? Only
when my sense of God is greater than my fear of
death can I stand before all that is "not subject"
without terror in my heart. If I expect God to save
me from the river that would draw me under and
cast me lifeless on its shore, then God and the river

will be enemies. But if God is greater than death, then God and the river can be friends.

If I fall into the river-not-subject and it pulls me under, I will die. But if I fall into God-not-subject and God pulls me under, I will be sustained, even in the depths, and emerge whole.

responding

You who are not subject,
into whose dark depths I peer,
your eddies and whirlpools frighten me.

I fear that should I fall into you
I would lose all control
and be sucked down to the darkness of death.

How can I trust you,
knowing this is so,
knowing this could happen?

Yet I cannot escape your pull,
and I know that standing on the edge
and holding back offers no real security.

For the darkness can find me
just when I think I am secure.

So help me to let go
and recognize that to you,
death is not death.

To be immersed in you
is not to escape from darkness,
but to enter it, not alone.

surrendering

Darkness is not dark to you.

Augustine of Hippo

6. The Call of the River

paying attention

I took the trail to the river because I wanted to see open water again after nothing but solid ice on the lakes, brittle frozen brush, and snow that felt like sand. I wanted to see something open and alive and listen to the gurgle of water as it rippled its way around the rocks of some open place that had never quite closed. I knew of such a place where in summer time a rapids whitened the blue of the South Kawishiwi. . . .

I skied to the very edge of the riffle and stood there, feasting my eyes and ears. Moving water after thirty or forty below when the whole world has seemed a frozen crystal of blue and white was an exciting thing. The river was alive and everything within it was alive. Bronze nuggets of gravel moved in the sunlight, and among them danced iridescent bits of shell, whirling madly for a moment only to settle and dance again. Sand eddied impatiently around the larger rocks, and as I watched I knew that, while all life now seemed dead beneath the surface, nothing had really changed. The river moved, blood still ran hot, and the endless cycle went on as before.

Sigurd Olson

There is within me a fierce desire to live that is as powerful as a river that refuses to freeze, even at forty below. Though the river is frozen everywhere, when we find that one open place, we glimpse the life that courses below its frozen surface. There we can contemplate the vital energy that flows even when all else seems frozen.

There is a place like that within me too, within all of us. It is the current of divine life within us, that little bit of hope that won't give up, that little spark of faith amidst the doubt. It beckons us when all seems frozen or dead. I hear its voice when a friend offers encouragement, when a coworker puts in more effort than required, when a stranger offers an unnecessary kindness. It speaks in the understanding and love of my family. This "moving water" within me is the movement of divine life.

Etty Hillesum, a young Jewish woman, drew strength from it when she would delight in the small patch of blue sky visible to her from her cell in a Nazi concentration camp. Julian of Norwich, a twelfth-century English mystic, encountered it in her hermitage, where even in the midst of an outbreak of the Black Death, she heard its voice telling her, "All will be well." It is always there, if I learn where to find it.

How do I find that open water
in the midst of the ice?
How do I hear your call?

In the depth of winter
I rely on my summer memories,
straining to recognize the trail's turns
hidden under the snow.

In the silence of the forest
the only sound is the wind.
Where is the faint voice of the river?

Let me search for the tracks of others
who seek to drink from the frozen stream.
Let me follow my heart's desire
believing it will not deceive me.

Let me move deliberately,
not fearing the future,
awake to the beauty around me,
alert to the voice that whispers,
"All will be well."

surrendering

I know not what may lie in wait for us. . . . And
yet I find life beautiful and meaningful.

Etty Hillesum

7. Moving in the River's Rhythm

paying attention

The ooze, the source of the great river, is now a white shoot tumbling over brown bellies of conglomerate rock. Wind throws seeds of water to another part of the mountainside; soft earth gives way under my feet, clouds spill upward and spit rain. Isn't everything redolent with loss, with momentary radiance, a coming to different ground? Stone basins catch the waterfall, spill it again; thoughts and desires strung together are laddered down.

To trace the history of a river or raindrop, as John Muir would have done, is also to trace the history of the soul, the history of the mind descending and arising in the body. In both, we constantly seek and stumble on divinity, which, like the cornice feeding the lake, and the spring becoming a waterfall, feeds, spills, falls, and feeds itself over and over again.

Gretel Ehrlich

pondering

In the rhythm of the river I discover the rhythm of my life. My beginning, too, was liquid—two cells colliding in a stream, swept together to a safe shore.

Doubling, doubling, doubling again, I grew, until finally the river of life carried me to birth.

With what momentary radiance, with what foreshadowing of loss did I come to this different ground?

The river continued to carry me as needs became words, words became thoughts, thoughts became desires. I let myself be carried and laughed. I struggled against the river's current and wept. I fought to escape the river and failed.

I do not fight the river so much anymore. I'm learning to trust it, to savor each passing vista of the shore. I'm growing in appreciation of my fellow river travelers. But still I struggle to stay afloat through the rapids, not completely trustful, or open, or grateful. As I trace the history of my soul, I remember all the stumbling and surprising ways I have encountered God, all of the diverse ways my soul has risen and descended in the ever present rhythm of grace.

responding

I cannot return to the source of my life,
against the current to the origin of the stream.
But I can imagine the raindrops that flowed
    together,
the rivulet at its first flowing,
the stream that gathered momentum
and was fed by other streams.

And I can remember the needs,
the words, the thoughts, and the desires
that shaped the history of my soul.
All the while my words and my desires,
my laughing and my crying,
were your words, your dreams;
your joys, your tears.

I was seeking you without knowing it,
always stumbling upon you without seeing it,
and still am today.
You, all the while, were the spring,
feeding the river of my life.

surrendering

My soul has grown deep like the rivers.

Langston Hughes

8. Carrying the River Within You

Many a time have I merely closed my eyes at the end of yet another troublesome day and soaked my bruised psyche in wild water, rivers remembered and rivers imagined. Rivers course through my dreams, rivers cold and fast, rivers well-known and rivers nameless, rivers that seem like ribbons of blue water twisting through wide valleys, narrow rivers folded up in layers of darkening shadows, rivers that have eroded deep down into a mountain's belly, sculpted the land, peeled back the planet's history exposing the texture of time itself. Rivers and sunlight, mountains and fish: they are always there, rising up out of exhaustion, a sudden rush of sound and motion. . . .

Harry Middleton

pondering

One day in early September, my son Peter and I rented a canoe and took a trip down the St. Joseph River. The cloudless sky was a rich, deep blue and the light breeze created just a soft ripple on the river's surface. Young turtles sunning themselves on logs plopped in the water as we glided by. We spied an occasional blue heron perched on the bank and a few swans moving gracefully through a pool.

The river was surprisingly empty of human presence. There were a few boys fishing under a highway bridge and a single pontoon boat. But they did not rob us of the sense that the river was ours, that on this river so close to home there was a quiet, peaceful world without the pressures and demands of our everyday life. I like to remember that day, not only for its quiet beauty, but to create a peaceful space within myself. I want to carry that day, that river, within me.

I close my eyes and I am there. The river becomes part of me and part of the bond between Peter and me. It flows through my mind, carving a path through my psyche, laying bare the texture of memory. I travel upstream and remember the joys and sorrows that have formed the course of my life. I am carried downstream as I recall the people, places, and things that I cherish, moving always toward the great sea to which every river flows.

When the river becomes a part of me, I sense my life as a whole rather than as scattered fragments; I know that there is a peaceful center which I need only take the time to connect with; I know that I come from somewhere and am going somewhere, that I am a part of something greater, that I belong to people and to places.

When you are bruised or troubled, let the river carry you. Close your eyes and go to that river, real or imagined, which is for you the river of life.

responding

You are always there,
flowing quietly, steadily, powerfully.
How often do I pass you without noticing,
glimpse you without remembering.

Now in this silent moment I think of you
and I find peace in you again,
like the swan swimming gracefully,
like the heron watching vigilantly.

Let me turn to you when I am weary
and be renewed by your silent presence.
Let me carry you within me
and not forget your beauty.

surrendering

We are lives interconnected at the core. Flowing from the same spring, the waters of divine life pulse through our beings.

Wendy Wright

the mountain

paying attention

With my stave I prop my pack upright and sit back against a mountainside, my face in cold shade and hot sun on my arms and belly. Pine needles dance in the light breeze against the three white sister peaks in the northwest. I sit in the burning hum of mountain bees. An emerald butterfly comes to my knee to dry its wings, its gold wings with black specks above, white polka dots beneath. Through the frozen atmosphere, the sun is burning.

In the clearness of the Himalayan air, mountains draw near, and in such splendor tears come quietly to my eyes and cool on my sunburned cheeks. This is not mere soft-mindedness, nor am I all that silly with the altitude. My head has cleared in these weeks free of intrusions—mail, telephones, people, and their needs—and I respond to things spontaneously, without defensive or self-conscious screens. Still, all this *feeling* is astonishing: not so long ago I could say truthfully that I had not shed a tear in twenty years.

Peter Matthiessen

There are no mountains here where I live. On the highway south of town there is a sign that marks the North/South Continental Divide. North of this unremarkable line the rivers flow into the Great Lakes; to the south they empty eventually into the Mississippi and flow into the Gulf. We are a long way from the Continental Divide in the Rockies that separates east from west, or even from the Appalachian divide for that matter. From here, one does not encounter a mountain without some effort. More often than not, I look down on them from an airplane window on the way to New York or California. Not the proper perspective. But when circumstances allow me to make the effort, I head to Colorado Springs where my sister-in-law Chris and her husband Mike live.

Pike's Peak towers over the city. At 14,110 feet, it is often snow capped when we arrive in early summer. They live almost at the foot of the mountain, and standing on their deck I get the proper perspective from which to encounter a mountain. Its sheer immensity calms me. I stare at it in amazement.

In the quiet I hear the whir of the hummingbirds and listen to the wind in the piñon pines and Russian olive trees. The mountain's stability and enormity are comforting. As I remember other moments of returning to this mountain from time to time, I recall what has changed in my life over the years. But the mountain is the same. Then I think of all the years of my life before I ever came to this place, and know that the mountain was the same then. And if I venture to think forward, I know that regardless of what may come, the mountain will be there.

By simply being there, mountains break down our defenses. We may come eager to the encounter, as I seem to do, or be caught unawares as Peter Matthiessen described. Their seeming permanence puts our frantic pace in perspective. Their ageless character offers us a different sense of time. And perhaps, if the moment is right, we too will transcend our self-consciousness and our defensiveness, perhaps we will experience a deeper dimension of our lives.

responding

You who dwell in the mountains
yet cannot be contained by them,
in your presence I realize
how unlike a mountain I am.

Your stillness reveals my frenetic pace,
your silence interrupts my noise,
your permanence punctuates my many
    changes.

Yet you do not draw me to yourself
simply to show me what I am not,
but to remind me of what I can be.

For my path does not lead me
through still and silent reaches of your timeless
    slopes,
but along busy, noisy roads where things are
    ever changing.

And it is just there that your pervasive
    presence
invites me to open my eyes,
to let myself feel and respond with genuine
    sincerity.

You who dwell in the mountains,
in your presence I am free
to accept the reality and gift of my life.

surrendering

The capacity for delight is the gift of paying attention.

Julia Cameron

paying attention

We were able to make out almost exactly where Everest should be; but the clouds were dark in that direction. We gazed at them intently through field glasses as though by some miracle we might pierce the veil. Presently the miracle happened. A whole group of mountains began to appear in gigantic fragments. Mountain shapes are often fantastic seen through a mist; these were like the wildest creation of a dream. A preposterous triangular lump rose out of the depths; its edge came leaping up at an angle of about seventy degrees and ended nowhere. To its left a black serrated crest was hanging in the sky incredibly. Gradually, very gradually, we saw the great mountainsides and glaciers and arêtes, now one fragment, now another through the floating rifts, until far higher in the sky than imagination had dared to suggest, the white summit of Everest appeared. And in this series of partial glimpses we had seen a whole; we were able to piece together the fragments, to interpret the dream. . . .

George Mallory

What is it that makes mountains so beautiful, so able to captivate us? Sir George Mallory expresses a bit of the beauty of Everest in these words. He was a man so possessed by Everest's beauty that he made three attempts to reach the summit. He died on the third try, and his body was only recently discovered, some seventy years later. We don't know if he ever made it to the summit.

One of the most arresting features of mountains is the way opposites coincide in them. Massive, weighty, powerful—yet delicate, fragile, graceful. They seem to be "hanging in the sky, incredibly . . . floating," as Mallory said. Another dimension of their beauty is their capacity to surprise us. Their unpredictability, their endless variety of shapes, the unimaginable, incredible way they hang there is "like the wildest creation of a dream." And mountains are beautiful in the way they capture and reflect the light. Radiant, glowing, almost translucent, their ethereal colors elevate us in body and soul. As we gaze on them we do indeed "pierce the veil" of the ordinary.

The beauty of life is like the beauty of the mountains. How often are our most cherished moments the times when opposites coincide. We must hold on and let go at the same time. Fail and succeed. See and not see. Die and be born.

Like the mountains, life is unpredictable, refusing to conform to some predetermined mold.

"Who could ever imagine this?" we wonder, when we have arrived in some new and wonderful place that we would never have set out for.

And like the mountains, our lives have the wondrous capacity to capture and reflect the light. Caught up in an energy, a transcendent force, in love, we reflect and amplify the radiant light of this divine presence to one another.

We hope that by some miracle we might pierce the veil. And the miracle happens.

responding

Isn't it strange
that what I most admire in mountains
I fail to appreciate in life?

Why must joy and sadness coincide?
Why are things so unpredictable and fragile?
Why must I wait for the light to shine on me?

I have much to learn
about letting opposites be,
about the surprising power of the
    unimaginable,
about catching and reflecting light.

Teach me to love the mountain's ways in me.
Teach me how to appreciate their beauty.

surrendering

Let the beauty we love be what we do.

Rumi

3. The Comfort of the Mountain

paying attention

After a series of switchbacks had lifted us seven hundred feet in less than a quarter of a mile, we stopped to rest by a stream that was alternately falling through the air and racing down the mountainside. Everywhere, from every slope, the Cascades cascade. Water shoots out of cracks in the rock, it falls over the edges of the cliffs, it foams, sprays, runs, and plunges pure and cold. Enough snow and rain fall up there to irrigate Libya, and when water is not actually falling from the sky the sun is melting it from alpine ice. Down the dark-green mountainsides go streamers of white water, and above the timberline water shines against the rock. In every depression is a tarn, and we had passed a particularly beautiful one a little earlier and, from the escarpment we're looking back at it now. It was called Hart Lake and was fed by a stream that, in turn, fell away from a high and deafening cataract. The stream was interrupted by a series of beaver ponds. All around these free-form pools were stands of alder, aspen, Engelmann spruce; and from the surrounding mountains, just under the summits, were glaciers and fields of snow.

John McPhee

Just outside of Glenwood Springs in Colorado there is a place called Hanging Lakes. The steep rocky trail that leads to it is quite busy. Featured in many of the guide books, it is a favorite hike of locals and visitors alike. The climb is fairly strenuous, especially for "flatlanders" unused to the altitude.

All the way up one is accompanied by a bounding stream that tumbles its way down to the Colorado River that runs at its base. The difficult climb is well worth the effort. At the top, one finds a calm and tranquil place. A shallow lake literally seems to hang on a lush ledge. The shelf offers a beautiful panorama of the surrounding mountains. The clear waters team with trout and a gentle waterfall stretches across the back of the lake like a curtain. In this tranquil setting people seem to speak in hushed tones, lingering after the climb to absorb its peace.

But one is drawn higher still by the sound of yet another waterfall, this one louder and stronger. A brief further climb reveals a graceful plume falling some forty feet into a broad pool that forms the source of the second falls. There is plenty of room to walk behind the cascade and to refresh oneself in its cool spray.

The comfort of this place, like the comfort of the place in the Cascades described by John McPhee, is found not only in the moment of first discovery. It is in knowing that it is there always. Even now, after leaving it, the mountain remains, a place of surpassing beauty and calm. As I go about my hectic life, so often forgetful of the reality of the natural world, it is there . . . as if waiting for me to remember and return. From time to time I do recall it, and when I do I discover that the stream and its falls have carved out a place in my memory, a place of refreshment and peace.

When I go there I remember the goodness of this earth and my need to find myself anew in it: to be drawn upward by its heights, to be bathed in its waters, to see my life reflected in its hidden pools.

responding

Let me go there now
to that place in my memory
of refreshment and beauty and peace.

There I will recall
the joy of the climb,
the cool spray of the falls,
the goodness of the earth.

There I will remember
the stillness of the hidden pond,
the clarity of its waters,
the comfort of belonging.

Then I will return
to the world in which I live
grateful for each moment,
knowing who I am.

surrendering

This is the use of memory; for liberation.

T. S. Eliot

4. Standing in Awe

paying attention

Elijah walked for forty days and forty nights until he reached Horeb, the mountain of God. There he went into the cave and spent the night in it. Then the word of Yahweh came to him saying, "What are you doing here, Elijah?" He replied, "I am filled with jealous zeal for Yahweh Sabaoth, because the sons of Israel have deserted you, broken down your altars and put your prophets to the sword. I am the only one left, and they want to kill me." Then he was told, "Go out and stand on the mountain before Yahweh." Then Yahweh himself went by. There came a mighty wind, so strong it tore the mountains and shattered the rocks before Yahweh. But Yahweh was not in the wind. After the wind came an earthquake. But Yahweh was not in the earthquake. After the earthquake came a fire. But Yahweh was not in the fire. And after the fire there came the sound of a gentle breeze. And when Elijah heard this, he covered his face with his cloak and went out and stood at the entrance of the cave.

1 Kings 19:8-13
(The Jerusalem Bible)

Where do we find the awe-inspiring presence of God? We find it in unexpected places, when it's not exactly what we are looking for. This was Elijah's experience.

Elijah was, quite literally, running for his life. The apostate Queen Jezebel was after him. At first, he simply fled the city and lay down in the desert to die. Alone and hopeless, he was ready to give up. But as he slept under a broom tree, an angel brought him bread and water and urged him to get up and make the long journey to Mt. Horeb—a forty day walk into the Sinai desert.

So Elijah went. We don't know whether he went willingly or grudgingly, but forty days was certainly plenty of time to mull over what to do about the death sentence hanging over him and whether to continue in this prophetic role. Finally he came to Mt. Horeb, also known as Mt. Sinai, Israel's sacred mountain.

There he is confronted with this soul-piercing question: "What are you doing here?" His response reveals a conflicted heart. He is both filled with "jealous zeal" and feeling dejected. He is angry at Israel's loss of faith, their siding with Jezebel, their murdering the prophets. Perhaps he even seeks revenge. But there is also the bitter taste of self-pity in his words: "I am the only one left, and they want to kill me." In other words, "Why have you abandoned me?"

"Go out and stand on the mountain before me," he is told. There he encounters a series of cataclysmic displays of divine power, just the type of display that Elijah had invoked to best the queen's prophets back in Israel, just the type of display that would have protected him when Jezebel started her manhunt: a wind like a tornado shattering rocks, an earthquake splitting open the mountain's side, a scorching fire consuming everything before it. But God was not in the wind, not in the earthquake, not in the fire. "So where are you then?" we can almost hear Elijah saying. And then there came the sound of a gentle breeze and Elijah covered his face, for he knew well that no one could look upon God and live.

How often do I, like Elijah, approach the mountain looking for something? I have questions to be answered, conflicts to be sorted out. I am angry and looking for justice, depressed and looking for solace. Every vista of the mountain's grandeur, its majesty, its power, fails to provide me with what I am looking for. The mountain does not yield to me, I must yield to the mountain. Like Elijah, standing on the mountain, I learn to wait: to listen carefully, to watch patiently. And when the storms have passed by, I discover the mountain on its own terms—in a quiet, gentle breeze. Then unexpectedly, I find what I was not looking for, and I stand in awe.

And then, like Elijah, I rise and return to my life.

What are you doing here on this mountain?

Looking for answers,
seeking inspiration,
hoping for comfort,
trying to escape.
But my answers are partial,
the inspiration, fleeting,
the comfort, incomplete,
the escape, foiled.

What are you doing here on this mountain?

Looking for something I cannot name,
but have seen in rare moments,
heard in faint calls,
felt in light breezes.
Something from which I hide my face
even while it calls me to come out.
Something that passes quietly,
stilling my unquiet mind.

Here on this mountain
I am waiting in silence,
hoping for presence,
standing in awe.

surrendering

The soul always stands ajar, ready to welcome the ecstatic experience.

Emily Dickinson

paying attention

The dark clouds came tumbling at the two climbers, slowly unfurling and rolling over, pushing ahead of them a mass of agitated and conflicting winds, so violent that they pressed back Rafi's beard and made him look like a goat. In one gust of wind they were hit with rain, snow, and hail, one rapidly following the other and then dried by the cold air blowing through their clothes until everything they wore ballooned out from them as if to tear away.

They struggled into oilskins as the first lightning bolt snaked down the precipice and raised their hair on end. Everything went white and they were thrown against the rock like fishing floats. Instant thunder rattled their skulls and reverberated out toward other mountain ranges for a minute or more. Even as it ceased, their ears were ringing and they could not see.

When their vision returned they saw dark clouds rising into the same sort of obliging curves in the pine trees on the ledges. The high front rushed west and made a wonderful, terrifying, obedient dip right above the two climbers as it crested and abandoned the spire, like a snake that takes a wall.

Mark Helprin

Few of us, certainly not me, have experienced anything like the storm on the mountain which Mark Helprin describes here. But there is something in the reservoir of our experience that evokes the feeling of powerlessness when we encounter a mountain.

Perhaps a mountain will confront me with a sense of inadequacy. I am a far cry from the strong and agile climbers described here, and always have been. Mountains can intimidate me. Perhaps the feeling will be one of raw fear. I may recoil at the prospect of standing on the ledge of a steep mountain slope, inches away from a fall. Or maybe the feeling I get is simply one of smallness. Standing before the immensity of a mountain, I recognize my littleness.

Real as these feelings of inadequacy, fear, and smallness are, there is another more profound feeling that transcends them. It is a sense of powerlessness. Confronting the full force of a storm on a fully exposed mountainside can bring one to this realization rather quickly. But so can the simple act of standing mindfully before a mountain.

Mountains have always been symbols of the divine. In many traditions they represent the mysterious and the holy, the transcendent aspect of God who is unknown and unknowable. They represent God's power, God's otherness. But recently feminist scholars have begun to discover another way that ancient religions viewed the mountains. Biblical scholars have begun to discover an alternate way of viewing the God of the mountains. The Hebrew name for God who dwelt in the mountains was *El Shaddai*. Scholars are tracing the linguistic origins of this rather masculine image of God back to an earlier feminine sense. *Shaddai,* some say, had its roots in the word for breast, and thus the mountain was once a symbol of nurture and care.

Our experience of powerlessness before a mountain is a complex one. It is true that we are filled with fear and trembling, but it is also true that we are nurtured and comforted. Powerlessness is unsettling, but there is a way in which it is also freeing. I think that is what Helprin's climbers discovered.

responding

On this obliging precipice
reveal to me
your terrifying, wonderful presence.

On this abandoned ledge
let the thunder of your voice
raise my hair on end,
let the lightning of your touch
blind my unseeing eyes.

And in the instant between
the lightning and the thunder
let the knowledge of your presence
roll over me like a storm.

Unfurl the dark cloud
of your unrelenting nearness.
Let the comfort of your wildness
rain down upon me.

surrendering

Never tread upon the top of a mountain.

A Buddhist admonition

6. The Call of the Mountain

⌒paying attention

I have always lived at altitude. My bones, long muscles, lung capacity came to me at 7,000 feet—at a place fallen east and slightly off the Yellowstone Plateau. I think that children who grow at high places are raised more by altitude than by their parents. I think the higher the home, the less we are body, the more we are spirit, and that our structure—gross and ethereal—benefits from the tutelage of a voice that does not speak our language, precisely, that the veil is dropped from the earth's face and she speaks to us plainly, to each atom, ensuring that absolutely nothing is lost in the translation, at high places, where the air is thin and her voice is freed to melody.

Mark Spragg

⌒pondering

In what language do the mountains speak to me? It is a spiritual language certainly, ethereal, calling me higher. But it is not a call in opposition to the material, not a call to rise above the earth. Rather it is a call to drop the veil from my eyes and see the earth's face plainly, to discover the spirit in her rocks, her trees, her summits. It is a call to let each living atom of the mountain speak to each living atom of my body. It is the call of a sweet melodious voice that beckons me to listen more deeply.

Never mind that I was not born at 7,000 feet. I hear the call nonetheless. Never mind that I did not hear it as a child, I hear it now. It calls me to learn a new language, a new way of knowing myself on this earth. It stirs in me a desire to become one with the earth, to live in harmony with it.

This is what it means to set out, to ascend to the heights. It is not a process of claiming a mountain, but of being claimed by it. It is not a journey to conquer, but to be conquered. It is not a call to stand upon a mountain top and look outward, but to stand in the presence of a mountain and look within.

responding

Drop the veil from my eyes
let me see you face to face.

Pierce the din with your song
let me hear your melody.

Claim me.
Conquer me.

Let each atom speak clearly,
let each atom penetrate.

surrendering

[M]ake] your life a worthy expression of leaning into the light.

Barry Lopez

7. Moving in the Mountain's Rhythm

paying attention

So many mornings waking I have seen her from the window before any other thing: dark against the daybreak, silvery in summer light, faint above river-valley fog. So many times I have watched her at evening, the faintest outline in mist, immense, remote, serene: the center, the central stone. "The stone is in the center," I wrote in a poem about her years ago. But the poem is impertinent. All I can say about her is impertinent.

When I was writing the first draft of this essay in California, on July 23, she erupted again, sending her plume to 60,000 feet. Yesterday, August 7, as I was typing the words, "the 'meaning' of eruption," I checked out the study window and there it was, the towering blue cloud against the northern sky—the fifth major eruption. How long may her labor be? A year, ten years, ten thousand? We cannot predict what she may, or might, or will do, now, or next, or for the rest of our lives, or ever. A threat; a terror; a fulfillment. This is what serenity is built on. This unmasks the metaphors. This is beyond us, and we must take it personally. This is the ground we walk on.

Ursula K. Le Guin

What is the rhythm of a mountain? We pay attention to our mountains, like compass points. But we don't have to keep track of them. There they are and there they'll stay. They do not move like the tides or the rivers, they do not shift like the desert's sand. They may, like the forests, change with the seasons. But the change on a mountain is not like the change we experience in the forest. Mountains change little, their movement is imperceptible. Their rhythm cannot be seen, even if we lived a thousand years.

The mountains seem to be stability itself. Even when we cannot see them we know that they are there, the serene center. We build the rhythms of our lives around such centers.

So what then, if our center, like Mount St. Helen's, cannot hold. What if it gives way not once, but repeatedly, with no end in sight? Our lives careen out of control. We live from moment to moment not knowing what will come next. The metaphors that make sense of our lives are unmasked, we are left speechless.

We shudder at such a possibility. It is indeed a terror, a threat, beyond our comprehension. But a fulfillment? The foundation of our serenity? What is this writer saying? What has the volcano taught her?

Such serenity or fulfillment would indeed be unlike any we have ever known. Is there a serenity that comes with the knowledge that the rhythm of our lives can be thrown off at any moment? Is there peace in the awareness that things could change irreparably without notice?

Such peace can only be the peace that surpasses understanding. Such tranquillity can only come to those who know that there is something beyond the mountain, that the metaphor is not the reality.

Only knowledge such as this, even if grasped dimly, unsurely, can be the ground that we walk on. Only such a still point can be the source of our rhythm.

responding

May such a thing never happen!
Yet every day I see it all around me:
lives explode like mountains,
familiar rhythms are swept away,
melted in lava, covered in ash.

When the center does not hold
what is there beyond the center?
In the midst of chaos
time careens madly, free-falling wildly
beyond terror, beyond understanding.

When all my metaphors are unmasked,
when the ground I walk on trembles,
can I sense in this heaving the labor pains of
     birth?
With so faint a hope, let me find my way.
In such unknowing, let me see but dimly.

surrendering

I lift up my eyes to the mountains, from whence
comes my help.

Psalm 121

⌒paying attention

[I]nman] unrolled the Bartram and held it to the yellow light and riffled through the pages till his eyes fell on a passage that caught his attention. It was this:

> The mountainous wildness I had lately traversed appeared regularly undulated as the great ocean after a tempest; the undulations gradually depressing, yet perfectly regular, as the squama of fish, or imbrications of tile on a roof; the nearest ground to me of perfect full green; next more glaucous; and lastly almost blue as the ether with which the most distant curve of the horizon seemed to be blended. . . .

A picture of the land Bartram detailed leaped dimensional into Inman's mind. Mountains and valleys on and on forever. A gnarled and taliped and snaggy landscape where man might be seen as an afterthought. Inman had many times looked across the view Bartram described. It was the border country stretching endlessly north and west from the slope of Cold Mountain. Inman knew it well. He had walked its contours in detail, had felt all its seasons and registered its colors and smelled its smells. . . . But to Inman's mind . . . the peaks now stood higher, the vales deeper than they did in truth. Inman imagined the fading rows of ridges standing pale and tall as cloudbanks, and he built the contours of them and he colored them, each a shade paler and bluer until, when he had finally reached the invented ridgeline where it faded into sky, he was asleep.

Charles Frazier

pondering

Inman is on a long journey home. Wounded in a Civil War battle, he walks out of the hospital and does not stop walking, always striving for his home on Cold Mountain. Along the way he is strengthened by memory of home and of the mountains that he reads in the only book he has had with him from the start, William Bartram's *Travels Through North and South Carolina*. The image of his mountain home "leaped dimensional" into his mind. But it was not a sudden recollection, for it was there all along. He had been carrying those mountains within him, an energizing, comforting, inspiring vision.

I, too, carry mountains within me: Bear Mountain, the mountain of my childhood; Machu Pichu, a place that became a part of my life during early adulthood; and Pike's Peak which has become important to me in recent years.

Bear Mountain lies on the west side of the Hudson River, some fifty miles north of New York City. As a child, it was the only mountain I ever knew. Each fall we would pack the car for an annual picnic. My sisters and brother and I would walk through its woods and explore its streams. It was a wondrous place, so different from the flat sandy terrain of Long Island where we were from. Bear Mountain is still with me.

As a young man I traveled to Peru. In the midst of a Spanish language immersion, I made a trip to the ancient Inca city of Machu Pichu. This ancient ceremonial city sits atop in a saddle between two peaks. Wayna Pichu rises high above it. I climbed to the top with a friend, and I remember still the thrill of standing upon it and looking out through clouds at the Andes and down some 2,000 feet to the Urambamba River below. It was a moment that in retrospect captures my sense of the sacred at that time—something that I could strive for and indeed grasp through practiced discipline and hard work. Machu Pichu is still with me.

These days, when I can stand in the shadow of Pike's Peak, I rediscover both my childlike wonder at a mountain and my youthful desire to scale its peaks. But I look at a mountain differently now, and my sense of spirituality is different too. It is not there for me to conquer. Certainly it is still a source of wonder, but I am not so young and naive. The mountain is a powerful presence, a sacred reality. Simply to be there is enough. I know now that I can't get where I want to go by climbing. I must simply pause, somewhere beyond wonder, and wait.

God is in the mountain, and the mountain is in God. And when I am near it, I am caught up in that interplay. It does not matter if I am on the summit or at the base. Just being near it is enough. Calling it to mind is enough, since now it is in me too.

When I do recall it, as when I recall Bear Mountain or Machu Pichu, I am again transported to an inner place where the presence of God surrounds and sustains me. It is a wondrous presence, it is a presence that calls me higher. Like Inman, I am sustained by it on my journey home.

responding

Mountains and valleys on and on forever
so goes my life from the wonder of childhood,
to the striving of youth,
to the restless searching of my adult years.

In the joy of discovery,
in the exhilaration of ascent,
in the silence of the mountain,
you have always been there.

You know the gnarled and taliped
landscape of my soul.
You have walked its contours,
felt all its seasons, registered its colors.

You, the ridgeline of my life,
gladden me with wonder,
lift me to your summit,
enshroud me in your silence.

surrendering

The mountains are our true home.

John Muir

Notes

Epigram

Rachel Carson, *The Sense of Wonder*, New York: Harper and Row, 1956.

1. Reading the Book of Nature

Chet Raymo, *Natural Prayers,* St. Paul, MN: Hungry Mind Books, 1999.

Scott Russell Sanders, *Writing From the Center,* Bloomington, IN: Indiana University Press, 1995.

James Finley, *The Contemplative Heart,* Notre Dame, IN: Sorin Books, 1999.

M. Basil Pennington, *Lectio Divina*, New York: Crossroad Publishing, 1998.

2. The Shore

Rachel Carson, *The Edge of the Sea*, Boston: Houghton Mifflin Company, 1955.

Anne Morrow Lindbergh, *Gift From the Sea*, New York: Random House, 1955.

Douglas Carlson, *At the Edge*, Fredonia, NY: White Pine Press, 1989.

Robert Kunzig, *The Restless Sea,* New York: W.W. Norton and Co., 1999.

Henry Beston, *The Outermost House: A Year of Life on the Great Beach of Cape Cod*, New York: Henry Holt and Company, 1928 and 1949.

Brenda Peterson, "Bread Upon the Waters" in *The Earth at Our Doorstep: Contemporary Writers Celebrate the Landscapes of Home,* edited by Annie Stine, San Francisco: Sierra Club Books, 1996.

Loren Eiseley, "The Star Thrower" in *The Unexpected Universe,* New York: Harcourt Brace & Company, 1969.

Walt Whitman, "The Shore Fancies" in *The Collected Writings of Walt Whitman, Vol. 1: Specimen Days,* New York: NYU Press, 1963.

3. The Forest

Thomas Berry, *The Dream of the Earth,* San Francisco: Sierra Club Books, 1988.

Belden Lane, *Landscapes of the Sacred*, Mahwah, NJ: Paulist Press, 1988.

Richard Nelson, *The Island Within*, New York: Vintage Books, 1991.

John Muir, "A Windstorm in the Forest," in *The Mountains of California,* New York: Penguin Nature Classics, 1997.

Bill Bryson, *A Walk in the Woods: Rediscovering America on the Appalachian Trail,* New York: Broadway Books, 1998.

Henry David Thoreau, *Walden*, New York: Vintage Books, 1991.

Bhikkhu Nyanasobhano, "Contemplation of a Once Tree," in *Orion*, Vol. 18, No. 1, Winter 1999.

Kathleen Dean Moore, *Riverwalking,* Minneapolis: The Lyons Press, 1995.

4. The Desert

Barry Lopez, *Desert Notes and River Notes*, New York: Avon Books, 1990.

T. E. Lawrence, *Seven Pillars of Wisdom*, New York: Penguin Books, 1979.

Tony Hillerman, *Skinwalkers*, New York: HarperCollins, 1986.

Carlo Carretto, "Why, O Lord?" in *Carlo Carretto: Selected Writings*, edited by Robert Ellsberg, Maryknoll, NY: Orbis Books, 1994.

Nouhou Agah, quoted in "Journey to the Heart of the Sahara," Donovan Webster, *National Geographic,* Vol. 195, No. 3 (March, 1999).

Geoffrey Moorhouse, *The Fearful Void*, New York: C. N. Potter, 1989.

Edmund Jabès, *From the Desert to the Book,* quoted in *The Sierra Club Desert Reader,* Gregory McNamee, editor, San Francisco: Sierra Club Books, 1995.

Terry Tempest Williams, *Desert Quartet: An Erotic Landscape,* New York: Pantheon Books, 1995.

5. The River

Hermann Hesse, *Siddhartha,* translated by Hilda Rosner, New York: New Directions, 1951.

David James Duncan, "The War for Norman's River," in *Sierra,* Vol. 83, No. 3 (May/June, 1998).

Ursula Hegi, *Stones from the River,* New York: Simon and Schuster, 1994.

Roger Housden, *Sacred Journeys in a Modern World,* New York: Simon and Schuster, 1998.

Wendell Berry, "The Rise" in *Recollected Essays 1965-1980,* New York: Farrar, Straus & Giroux, 1981.

Sigurd F. Olson, "The River" in *The Singing Wilderness,* Minneapolis: University of Minnesota Press, 1997.

Gretel Ehrlich, *Islands, the Universe, Home,* New York: Viking Penguin, 1991.

Harry Middleton, *Rivers of Memory,* Boulder, CO: Pruett Publishing Co., 1993.

6. The Mountain

Peter Matthiessen, *The Snow Leopard,* New York: Viking Penguin, 1978.

George Mallory, 1921 quoted in *Everest,* edited by Peter Giolman, London: Little, Brown, and Co., 1993.

John McPhee, excerpt from "A Mountain" in *Encounters with the Archdruid,* New York: Farrar, Straus & Giroux, 1971.

Mark Helprin, *A Soldier of the Great War,* New York: Avon Books, 1992.

Mark Spragg, "Singing in the High Places," in *Echoes of the Summit,* selected and edited by Paul Schullery, San Diego: Tahibi Books, Harcourt Brace & Company, 1996.

Ursula K. Le Guin, "A Very Warm Mountain," in *The Norton Book of Nature Writing,* New York: W.W. Norton Co., 1990.

Charles Frazier, *Cold Mountain,* New York: Atlantic Monthly Press, 1997.

Contributors

Nouhou Agah is weather officer in Bilma, Niger.

Thomas Berry, S.J. is the founder and director of the Riverdale Center for Religious Research in New York. Building on the work of Teilhard de Chardin, Berry seeks to bridge the gulf between science and theology, so much so that he is sometimes called a "geologian." His work is concerned with telling "the new story of the universe" in a way that finds theological significance in evolution and recognizes environmental activism as a spiritual task. Among his most important works are *The Dream of the Earth* and *The Great Work.*

Wendell Berry is a farmer, novelist, poet, essayist, and leader of the environmental movement. His writings reflect his abiding concern with human attentiveness to the natural world and our interaction with it in respectful and mutually enhancing ways. Among his many books are *The Unsettling of America: Culture and Agriculture,* his novel *The Memory of Old Jack,* and his collection of poems *A Timbered Choir: The Sabbath Poems (1979-1997).*

Henry Beston (1888-1968) was thirty-eight years old when he spent a year in a dune cottage on the Great Beach of Cape Cod in 1926. *The Outermost House* is a classic in the "solitary sojourn" genre of nature writing. Prior to this, his best known work, he had written an account of his service during World War I and two books of fairy tales. He went on to write other works on nature including *White Pine and Blue Water, Northern Farm,* and *The St. Lawrence.*

Bill Bryson spent twenty years in England before returning to the United States and settling in Hanover, New Hampshire. His writings about his travels around the world are noted for their humor and for their common touch. *A Walk in the Woods,* an account of his attempt to hike the Appalachian Trail, was a longtime bestseller and gained him a national audience. *I'm a Stranger Here Myself* is a lighthearted look at American life. His other books include *The Lost Continent: Travels in Small Town America, Neither Here Nor There: Travels in Europe,* and *In a Sunburned Country.*

Carlo Carretto (1910-1988) was raised in a devout family in Northern Italy. His work as an educator led to clashes with the Fascist regime, and he soon became involved in the Catholic Action Movement. Carretto was soon drawn to the spirituality of Charles de Foucauld, a French monk and founder of the Little Brothers of Jesus, a community dedicated to lives of hidden service and presence among the poor. As a lay brother in this community, Carretto followed the example of Foucauld in both Italy and the Sahara. Among his many books are *The God Who Comes, Letters From the Desert,* and *I, Francis.*

Douglas Carlson is an essayist whose works have appeared in journals such as *The American Literary Review, Adirondac,* and *The Georgia Review.*

Rachel Carson (1907-1964) originally intended to become a writer, but early on she changed her focus to biology. In 1932 she received her M.A. from Johns Hopkins University and pursued postgraduate studies at the Marine Biological Laboratory in Woods Hole, Massachusetts. Her article in *The Atlantic Monthly* in 1937 served as the basis for her first book, *Under the Sea-Wind.* In 1936 she began her career as an aquatic biologist with the U.S. Bureau of Fisheries and in 1940 went on to work for the U.S. Fish and Wildlife Service until 1952, the last three years as editor in chief of the service's publications. Her second book, *The Sea Around Us*, won a National Book Award in 1951. She went on to write *The Edge of the Sea* and in 1962 the book for which she is best known, *Silent Spring.* She died of cancer at the age of fifty-six.

David James Duncan, an environmental activist, is the author of the novel *The River Why* and a book of essays entitled *River Teeth.*

Gretel Ehrlich is a Wyoming rancher, a Buddhist, and a writer. She says in the preface of her 1985 book *The Solace of Open Spaces* that she was at last "able to take up residence on earth with no alibis, no self-promoting schemes." Among her other works are *Questions of Heaven* and *Islands, the Universe, Home.*

Loren Eiseley (1907-1977) was an anthropologist, educator, and author of more than twelve books. A native of Nebraska, he received his bachelor's degree from the University of Nebraska in 1933 and his master's and doctorate from the University of Pennsylvania where he served in various academic capacities for thirty years. His writings on anthropology covered a wide range of issues relating to evolution and its implications for humanity. Both scholarly and accessible, they have been praised as well for their poetic style. Best known among his books are *The Immense Journey, The Firmament of Time,* and *The Unexpected Universe.*

Charles Frazier grew up in the mountains of North Carolina, the setting of his novel *Cold Mountain.* Among the many things it was praised for is its eloquent expression of the role of place in human consciousness. The book won the National Book Award in 1997.

Ursula Hegi lived in a small German town until the age of eighteen when she moved to the United States. Her six novels and one collection of short stories focus on life in Germany and the effect of Nazism upon its people. "The older I get," she has said, "the more I realize that I am inescapably encumbered with the heritage of my country's history." Her most recent book is *The Vision of Emma Blau.*

Mark Helprin grew up in New York's Hudson Valley, attended Harvard, and spent two years in the Israeli army. His novels, *A Soldier of the Great War* and *Memoir From Antproof Case,* have received wide critical acclaim.

Hermann Hesse (1877-1962), a German novelist and poet, explored the relationship of people and nature in his early novels like *Peter Camenzind.* In his most popular works, which included *Siddhartha* and *Steppenwolf,* he offered hope to a nation disenchanted by World War I and celebrated the quest for identity and spirituality. Ostracized due to his pacifism in the face of Nazism, he lived out his life in Switzerland.

Roger Housden's varied career has included work as a management consultant and therapist in a cancer center. He is the founder of The Open Gate, a center in England that has brought innovative religious perspectives to Britain. He is the author of six books, including *Travels Through Sacred India* and *Retreat: Time Apart for Silence and Solitude.*

Tony Hillerman was raised in rural Oklahoma where his playmates were Seminole and Potawatomi children. After attending Oklahoma State University and serving in the military during World War II, he became a journalist. His career as a mystery writer began in 1970 with the publication of *The Blessing Way*. Since then he has published thirteen novels, most of which reveal the life and traditions of the Navajo Nation. He has received numerous awards for his writing, but regards his "Special Friend to the Dineh Award" as the most meaningful.

Edmund Jabès (1912-1991) was born in Cairo where he lived until 1957 when he was exiled from Egypt because he was a Jew. He settled in Paris and published three books of poetry and other works of philosophy.

Robert Kunzig is European editor of *Discover* magazine. His writing on the ocean has won wide acclaim. He believes that "This is a special moment in the history of our bond with the sea. Our view of it is very different from what it was just a few decades ago."

Belden C. Lane writes about the influence of landscape on spirituality. A professor of theological and American studies at St. Louis University, he is the author of *Landscapes of the Sacred: Geography and Narrative in American Spirituality* and *The Solace of Fierce Landscapes: Exploring Desert and Mountain Spirituality*.

T. E. Lawrence (1888-1935) was a British archaeologist who found himself caught up in the Arab struggle for emancipation from the Turks during World War I. He served as a military strategist to the Arabs and is best known for his account of the war told in *Seven Pillars of Wisdom*.

Ursula K. Le Guin is widely acclaimed for her science fiction writing. Her works in this genre include *The Left Hand of Darkness, The Lathe of Heaven*, and the *Earthsea* trilogy. The essay "A Very Warm Mountain" was written from her home in Portland, Oregon, where she watched Mount St. Helens erupt in 1980.

Anne Morrow Lindberg (1906-2001) may be best known today for her perennially popular book *Gift From the Sea,* published in 1956. It was her marriage to Charles Lindbergh in 1929 and the kidnapping and murder of their son Charles III in 1932 that kept her in the public eye earlier in her life. She is the author of eleven books, including numerous volumes of her letters and diaries. Her early books, *North to the Orient, Listen! The Wind,* and *The Steep Ascent,* all draw on her experience as an aviator using her travels as a metaphor for the search for inner balance. A graduate of Smith College, she and Charles eventually had six children. She is a member of the National Women's Hall of Fame and the National Aviation Hall of Fame.

Barry Lopez writes about the way the natural world and human culture shape and interact with each other. He has been a full-time writer since 1970 with seven fiction works, four collections of essays, and two nonfiction books published. His *Arctic Dreams: Imagination and Desire in a Northern Landscape* won the National Book Award in 1986.

George Mallory (1886-1924) made three attempts to ascend Everest. He was lost on the third expedition in 1924. His body was finally discovered in 1999. It is not known whether he actually ever reached the summit.

Peter Matthiessen has traveled throughout the world giving voice to the spirit of the wild in exotic places like Nepal, Kenya, the Northwest Territories, and in ordinary places close to home. Among his most widely acclaimed novels are *At Play in the Fields of the Lord* and *Far Tortuga. The Snow Leopard* won the National Book Award in 1978. He currently lives in East Hampton on Long Island where he continues to write and teach Zen Buddhism.

John McPhee is considered to be a pioneer of "new journalism." While his writing covers a wide variety of subjects, much of his work focuses on the natural world and environmental topics. Among his twenty-three nonfiction books are *The Pine Barrens*, a study of one of the few remaining wild areas of New Jersey, and *Encounters with the Archdruid* in which he profiles the radical leader of the Sierra Club, David Brower. McPhee lives and teaches in Princeton, New Jersey.

Harry Middleton (1949-1993) was a journalist and author of numerous award-winning books. His articles appeared in magazines and journals including *Smithsonian, Outside*, and *Sports Illustrated*. Among his books are *The Earth Is Enough* and *On the Spine of Time*.

Kathleen Dean Moore teaches philosophy at Oregon State University. Her book *Riverwalking* is a collection of her writings on the relationship between nature and philosophy.

Geoffrey Moorhouse is an adventurer and author of numerous books, the best known being *The Fearful Void*. In it he chronicles his attempt to cross the Sahara from the Atlantic to the Nile, a thirty-six-hundred-mile journey. After six months and some two thousand miles traveled, he concluded his quest in Tamanrasset, Algeria.

John Muir (1838-1914) was born in Dunbar, Scotland, immigrated to the United States in 1849, and grew up on a farm in Wisconsin. His study of the natural sciences at the University of Wisconsin led him to travel and explore nature throughout the world. He is most closely associated with California and Yosemite, which he fought to preserve. His articles in *Century* magazine were the basis of his book *The Mountains of California*. He founded the Sierra Club in 1892.

Richard Nelson writes on cultural anthropology and nature. Two of his books, *Hunters of the Northern Ice* and *Make Prayers to the Raven*, focus on the native people of Alaska. *The Island Within* won the John Burroughs award for nature writing in 1991.

Bhikkhu Nyanasobhano has been an actor and a playwright and is now an American Buddhist monk living in Chicago. He is the author of *Landscapes of Wonder: Discovering Buddhist Dhamma in the World Around Us*.

Sigurd F. Olson (1899-1982) was a pioneer of the environmental movement in the United States. A founding member and eventual president of The Wilderness Society, Olson spent much of his life in northern Minnesota. The forests and lakes of that region are the setting in which he reflects on our place in nature, and "that ancient realization of oneness." Olson did not begin his writing career until he was well into his thirties. Among his many books are *The Singing Wilderness, Listening Point, The Lonely Land,* and *Runes of the North.*

Brenda Peterson is the author of three novels and two collections of nature essays. Most recently she collaborated with co-editors Linda Hogan and Deena Metzger on *Intimate Nature: The Bond Between Women and Animals.* She lives on Puget Sound in Washington.

Mark Spragg has written for various publications including *Quest, Gray's Sporting Journal,* and *Northern Lights.* A native of Wyoming, he is also a poet, novelist, and screenwriter.

Henry David Thoreau (1817-1862) is perhaps America's most influential nature writer. Like his friend Ralph Waldo Emerson, he was a central figure in the Transcendental Movement. A jack-of-all-trades and a prolific writer, only two of his books were published during his lifetime: *A Week on the Concord and the Merrimack Rivers* and *Walden; or, Life in the Woods.* He died of tuberculosis at the age of forty-five.

Walt Whitman (1819-1892) was born on Long Island where he grew up with a love of nature and the sea. As a journalist in Brooklyn, he wrote about the life of the city and spoke out against slavery. His collection of poetry, *Leaves of Grass,* was self-published in 1855 and continually revised and expanded throughout his life. *Specimen Days,* published in 1882, is a multi-volume collection of his prose writings over an extended period.

Terry Tempest Williams says she writes "through my biases of gender, geography, and culture. . . . I am a woman whose ideas have been shaped by the Colorado Plateau and the Great Basin . . . these ideas are then sorted out through the prism of my culture—and my culture is Mormon." Among her works are *Refuge* and *An Unspoken Hunger.* She is Naturalist in Residence at the Utah Museum of Natural History in Salt Lake City.

ROBERT M. HAMMA, the author of eight
books including *Landscapes of the Soul*, holds
a Master's in Theology from the University
of Notre Dame as well as a Master's in
Divinity. He currently serves as the editorial
director of Ave Maria Press and its imprint
SORIN BOOKS. His last book, *Through
Good Times and Bad,* a book of reflections
on marriage, was cowritten with his wife,
Kathryn Schneider. They live with their
three children in Granger, Indiana.